Resilient Echoes

Resilient Echoes:

A Journey From Injustice To Empowerment

by

Brian Banks

Echoes of Resilience
Ghotchu Technologies LLC

Published by Independently Published
Publication Date: December 18, 2023
Language: English
ISBN-13: 979-8872178859

Library of Congress Cataloging-in-Publication Data is available upon request.

Printed in United States

First Edition

In the quiet before the storm, there is often a moment of reflection, a pause before life unfolds in ways we never anticipated. This book is born from such a moment, from a journey that began in the depths of injustice and led to a path of profound transformation.

My story, while unique in its details, echoes the experiences of many who have faced unimaginable challenges, who have been forced to navigate the turbulent waters of adversity and misjudgment. Yet, it is also a story of hope, resilience, and the unyielding power of the human spirit.

As you turn these pages, you will walk with me through the darkest of times, through the struggle and pain that came with a wrongful conviction that threatened to define my existence. But more importantly, you will witness the emergence of strength, understanding, and an unshakeable resolve to transform pain into a force for positive change.

This is not just my story. It reflects the universal struggle against injustice and the pursuit of a life rebuilt on the foundations of hope and perseverance. Each chapter is a testament to the indomitable human spirit and a guide to finding empowerment in the most unlikely places.

So, as you embark on this Exploration with me, remember that this is more than a story. It's a shared experience, a collective journey towards understanding, healing, and empowerment. My journey, in its essence, is a call to all who have faced, or will face, trials that seem insurmountable. It's a reminder that even in the darkest moments, there is a light that guides us towards a future filled with possibilities.

Welcome to an exploration of transformation. Welcome to the story of turning pain into empowerment.

Table of Contents

Chapter On
The Shock of an Unwanted Experience

Life has a curious way of presenting its most profound lessons through unexpected trials. For me, it was an unforeseen detour that served as the catalyst. A rude awakening shattered my preconceived notions of justice and fairness, and it put my inner strength to the test. As I faced a labyrinth of legal battles and the glaring eyes of public scrutiny, I found myself standing on the trembling ground of an identity that I had once believed to be unshakeable.

The upheaval distorted my perception of time; days dragged on, yet my emotions ran rampant, refusing to be tamed. The harsh reality brought a deluge of questions that went beyond the surface of the current crisis, probing the depths of my beliefs and self-concept. It was a period of profound questioning, a prelude to the evolution that awaited.

As I grappled with the fallout, I recognized that this was not merely a disruption but a profound transformation in progress. The sense of loss was palpable, extending from the immediate grasp of control to the broader understanding of my place in the world. With each passing day, the future I had meticulously planned appeared to disintegrate, paving the way for an uncertain but open horizon.

The confrontation with my new reality required an active engagement with the deeper, often unexplored, chambers of my psyche. It was a time for introspection, not just to seek refuge from the tempest but to find a new keel for my ship amidst the tumultuous sea. I began to peel back the layers of my identity, examining and challenging the long-held beliefs and narratives that had, until now, directed the course of my life.

As I delved deeper into self-reflection, it became clear that the true challenges lay within the narratives I had internalized over the years. These internal dialogues about my worth and identity had the power to anchor me to a bygone era or to catapult me into a future filled with new potential. It was time to author a fresh narrative, one that embraced the unwritten possibilities of the chapters ahead.

The journey ahead laid out a path strewn with the wrestling of old and new narratives, each tussle forging resilience within me. I came to understand that true strength was not about holding tightly to the known but about embracing the potential of the unknown. It was the start of an active exploration, a deliberate stride from a place of vulnerability toward empowerment.

Empowerment began to take root as I envisioned my purpose and identity in this new context. It involved more than mere bravery; it was a deep dive into vulnerability, courageously facing my fears, doubts, and perceived weaknesses. I came to see strength as an evolving process, one of constant learning, adapting, and overcoming.

This transformational period led to two pivotal realizations that guided my path forward. Firstly, I came to understand resilience in a new light. Far from being an innate trait, it emerged as a skill, meticulously crafted in the fires of adversity. It meant not just enduring challenges but actively engaging with them, extracting wisdom and growth from their depths. This shift in perspective from passive endurance to active engagement marked a significant turning point in my journey.

Progressing further, the second realization underscored the critical role of authenticity. It became evident that during external judgments and misconceptions, firmly grasping my true self was an act of both defiance and self-preservation. This stage was about stripping away imposed narratives to reveal my authentic identity, a task that involved not only discarding false labels but also fully embracing the intricacies of my personal story.

This phase of my journey transcended mere intellectual understanding, evolving into a profound emotional process that redefined my self-perception and my relationship with the world around me. It necessitated a delicate balance between self-compassion and critical reflection, a balancing act that involved both acknowledging the pain of my circumstances and actively seeking the growth opportunities they presented.

Emboldened by these realizations, I found that the resilience I had been nurturing became a cornerstone of my empowerment. It equipped me to not only address the immediate complexities of my situation but also to grapple with broader, more existential questions. This evolving resilience was a living testament to the potential for growth and transformation, even amidst the most daunting challenges.

As I progressed, the pursuit of authenticity, despite its inherent difficulties, proved to be profoundly rewarding. I learned to embrace vulnerability, not as a weakness but as a wellspring of strength. Acknowledging my fears and doubts became a practice of turning these emotions into catalysts for personal growth. This pursuit transcended personal development; it morphed into a guiding light for others, offering insights and strategies to navigate through their own complex journeys. The pathway to authenticity thus transformed from a solitary quest into a shared narrative, providing solace and inspiration to those who also found themselves at life's unpredictable crossroads.

Moving forward, I began to see these realizations not as final destinations but as milestones on an ever-evolving journey of self-discovery and growth. They became the guiding lights, influencing my reactions to new challenges and informing my decisions. This phase was characterized by an increasing commitment to authenticity and an understanding of the transformative power of resilience. It was about leveraging these principles to turn challenges into steppingstones, fostering personal growth and a deeper understanding of my life's purpose.

As this journey unfolded, it was punctuated by moments of profound insight and significant personal transformation. Each challenge I faced, each hurdle I overcame, added a distinct chapter to my life's narrative. This process enriched my story, making it far more intricate and profound than I had previously realized. It became evident that the complexities and trials of life were not just obstacles but opportunities to write a richer, more meaningful personal history.

As I advanced on this path, I discovered that the journey of overcoming adversity was far from straightforward. It was a tapestry woven with threads of doubt and despair yet interspersed with invaluable moments of clarity and empowerment. These experiences taught me the importance of patience – the realization that true growth and understanding evolve incrementally, marked by small, often subtle shifts rather than sudden transformations.

This phase of my journey also brought into sharp focus the immense power of perspective. I learned that the lens through which we view our circumstances can dramatically alter our experiences. Embracing a shifted perspective allowed me to perceive my challenges not solely as sources of pain but as opportunities for profound growth and heightened self-awareness. This reorientation was not a denial of my reality; rather, it was an active search for meaning and purpose amidst the turmoil. It became a conscious choice to find value in my experiences, transforming them from mere hardships into vital chapters of my personal evolution.

As I journeyed further, the value of human connection emerged as a pivotal aspect of my growth. Engaging with others, sharing my experiences, and listening to their stories, I found a sense of belonging and shared purpose. This phase of my journey underscored that while each of our stories is unique, they collectively weave into the broader human tapestry of resilience and perseverance.

Progressing, I also discovered the crucial role of proactive action and advocacy. I began to use my personal experiences as a platform to advocate for change and support others facing similar challenges. This transition from personal healing to active advocacy marked a significant evolution in my journey, transforming my individual struggle into a broader mission for justice and positive change.

In the subsequent phase of my path, the resilience and authenticity I had cultivated became the driving forces in reshaping my life. They guided my decisions and actions, aiding me in navigating the intricacies of reconstructing my identity and life. This stage was more than a recovery; it was a renaissance - an opportunity to build a life that truly resonated with my authentic self, unshackled from previous constraints and misconceptions.

As my journey unfolded, it began to intersect with broader societal issues, turning into an exploration of human resilience amidst systemic challenges. This new phase brought into focus the often-unseen internal battles that silently shape lives, offering a broader perspective on the universal nature of such struggles.

In this expanded realm of experience, my personal journey resonated with a collective human search for truth and meaning amidst turmoil. This period taught me that the most daunting challenges are often cloaked in the guise of insurmountable obstacles yet hidden within them are opportunities for profound growth and self-realization.

Advancing further, my path became intertwined with the larger quest for human dignity and understanding in adversity. This stage reinforced the importance of steadfastly adhering to personal values and beliefs, especially when confronted with challenging situations. It was a testament to the strength found in staying true to oneself, even under the most trying circumstances.

In this later stage of my journey, the focus shifted towards deriving meaning from the struggles I faced. This process involved transforming the pain and injustices I endured into foundations of strength and wisdom. It underscored a crucial life lesson: the essence of strength is not in avoiding the fall, but in the courage to rise again and again.

Further along the path, the role of community and the value of connections in our lives came to the forefront. This realization highlighted that our individual stories are part of a much larger narrative, woven together by shared experiences of adversity, resilience, and hope. It was a profound recognition of our interconnectedness and the collective strength that arises from it.

As I delved deeper into this phase, the importance of empathy and compassion became more pronounced. These qualities transcended mere emotional responses, evolving into fundamental principles that guided my interactions and worldview. Through this lens of empathy and compassion, my personal struggles transformed, offering new opportunities for meaningful connections and collective growth.

As I moved further along my path, I realized that the harsh experiences we endure have the potential to be transformative, not just for ourselves, but for those around us as well. This understanding revealed the far-reaching impact of our personal growth, creating a ripple effect that extends our lessons and strengths to others.

With the resilience I had developed, I found a new purpose in inspiring and guiding others. Sharing the narratives of my struggles and victories became a way to illuminate paths for those in similar situations, fostering a community bound by shared experiences and mutual understanding.

Progressing through my journey, I also came to deeply appreciate the moments of joy and peace that shone through the darkness. These fleeting instances were not just breaks in the storm but profound reminders of the enduring beauty and strength within us and the world around us. They reinforced the human capacity for hope and joy, even in the most challenging times.

As I progressed further, it became evident that the process of self-discovery and growth is an unending one. Every encounter, challenge, and victory I experienced was another step in a continuous journey of learning and transformation. This phase of my journey emphasized the need for ongoing reassessment and refinement of my beliefs, values, and objectives.

In this stage, I learned that the essence of my lessons went beyond mere survival in the face of adversity; they were about thriving amidst it. I began to see my struggles as opportunities to imbue my life and the lives of others with meaning, using these experiences to fuel positive change and growth.

Navigating through this part of my journey, I found myself painting a new understanding of life on the canvas of my experiences. The adversities I faced served to highlight the complexity and richness of the human experience, encompassing the depths of despair and the heights of triumph, and the enduring resilience that connects these extremes.

As I continued to navigate my journey, I discovered that our most profound strengths often surface during our most difficult times. It became clear that the trials of adversity are fertile grounds for uncovering and testing parts of our character that might otherwise remain dormant. These moments of discovery went beyond personal achievements, echoing a universal narrative of human resilience and success.

With each new step, the resilience and authenticity I had nurtured became integral tools for navigating the complexities of life. These qualities helped me develop a deeper sense of purpose and a clearer vision for my future. This newfound clarity acted not just as a goal but as a beacon, guiding me through new challenges and opportunities that arose.

This part of my journey also brought a deep recognition of the interconnectedness of our individual stories. I realized that, although unique in its details, my journey was part of a larger, shared human experience. This realization highlighted that our collective quests for meaning, belonging, and purpose are the threads that bind our stories together, offering solidarity and strength in the shared fabric of our lives.

As my journey evolved, the transformation I experienced began to transcend personal growth, expanding into a broader contemplation of our collective role in society. I came to understand that our capacity for change extends far beyond our personal spheres. We hold the power to influence and inspire others through our stories, our deeds, and our steadfast dedication to truth and justice. This phase of my journey was marked by an increasing awareness of the potential impact of individual actions on the larger social fabric.

Chapter Two
Bearing The Burden Of Misjudgment

The shadow of judgment, often clouding the soul's vibrancy, became for me a harsh teacher through my wrongful conviction. This experience, while fraught with challenges, revealed an underlying opportunity for transformation. It was a call to not just endure but to actively reshape my identity and emerge stronger, more authentic.

Confronted with a distorted image of myself, cast by a flawed system and public opinion, I realized the potential for profound personal growth. This journey wasn't merely about rejecting others' false perceptions. It involved a deeper exploration of my true self, leading to a redefined, unblemished sense of identity.

Amidst the isolation borne from misjudgment, a crucible for introspection emerged. In solitude, I faced and understood my deepest fears and insecurities. These moments of quiet reflection became catalysts, guiding me towards embracing my authentic self and forging a narrative rooted in genuine strength.

Creating a new narrative was an essential step in reclaiming my story. This task demanded not just a rejection of the false labels placed upon me, but a deeper, more courageous journey to redefine my identity. It involved embracing the full spectrum of my humanity, acknowledging my flaws, and recognizing my strengths. This process of self-redefinition harnessed the pain of being misjudged as a powerful impetus for personal growth and a deeper understanding of my place in the world.

The emotions that arise in response to judgment – anger, sorrow, frustration – while challenging, offered profound insights. I learned the significance of engaging with these emotions constructively. Mindfulness became a crucial practice, allowing me to observe and understand my feelings without being overwhelmed by them. This approach prevented negative emotions from eroding my inner strength, teaching me to use them as tools for insight and personal development.

The concept of resilience evolved for me during this journey. Far from merely being a defensive mechanism against adversity, resilience emerged as a transformative force. It shaped how I responded to challenges, altering my perceptions, and guiding my growth. This inner evolution was a process of turning the adversity of misjudgment into a foundation for growth and self-improvement, a true metamorphosis that reshaped my understanding of myself and my capabilities.

The path forward, emerging from judgment's shadow, involved navigating the complex interplay of doubt and self-assurance. This transformative journey was far from direct; it was rich with opportunities for deep, personal enlightenment.

It was in the aftermath of my wrongful accusation, in moments of quiet reflection, that I found the space to listen to my inner voice. This introspection revealed truths about my identity, worth, and untapped potential, guiding me toward a more assured sense of self.

Engaging in this internal dialogue meant confronting not just the external narratives imposed upon me but also challenging the internal doubts that echoed within. This process was akin to sifting through layers of identity, separating external impositions from the core of my authentic self. It demanded relentless self-exploration and the courage to face uncomfortable truths, leading to a more genuine and grounded understanding of who I am.

Central to this journey was the concept of forgiveness. Embracing forgiveness was not an act of excusing the wrongs done to me but a means of freeing myself from lingering bitterness and resentment. It was a crucial step towards achieving inner peace and readiness to move forward. In this act of forgiving, I discovered a form of empowerment – a reclamation of agency not to rewrite the past but to positively shape my future. Forgiveness thus became a transformative tool, enabling me to let go of what was and embrace what could be.

This part of my story highlights the crucial balance between individual empowerment and the need for systemic change. It became clear that personal growth and societal reform are not mutually exclusive; they are interconnected. My journey underscored the importance of not only transforming my own life but also contributing to the broader movement for justice reform. This approach went beyond personal healing; it was about playing a part in creating a more just and equitable society for others.

As my narrative unfolded, it was marked by significant moments of self-affirmation and realizations. Each step on this path was more than progress; it was a stance against the unjust labels I had been given and a testament to the enduring strength of my spirit. These moments weren't just milestones; they were acts of resistance and celebrations of the resilience inherent in my journey.

Emerging from the trials I faced, I gained a new perspective, a clarity born from enduring and overcoming adversity. This newfound clarity became the bedrock for reconstructing my identity and purpose. It mirrored the experiences of many who have endured wrongful convictions, each with their unique story, yet all sharing a universal narrative of struggle and the pursuit of justice. Their collective stories and mine reflect the resilience and longing for truth that binds us as humans.

The experience of Marcellus Williams, brought to light by the Innocence Project, exemplifies the challenges and triumphs in the journey towards justice. Williams' exoneration, achieved through the emergence of new DNA evidence, highlighted the critical role of perseverance and advocacy in challenging systemic failures. His prolonged struggle for justice, despite clear evidence of innocence, underlines the resilience required in the face of legal and bureaucratic obstacles.

Stories of individuals like Huwe Burton and Rafael Ruiz further reinforce this narrative. Their wrongful convictions and subsequent decades-long imprisonment, followed by exoneration, illustrate not just the failings of the justice system but also the extraordinary fortitude and persistence of those wrongfully convicted. Their experiences, while marked by unjust hardship, also showcase an incredible spirit of resilience and determination.

These stories of exoneration collectively underscore the importance of persistent advocacy and the need for systemic legal reforms. The efforts of the Innocence Project, leading to the freedom of over 240 individuals, extend beyond mere statistics. They represent profound shifts in individual lives and contribute to the ongoing dialogue about justice and legal reform. These narratives not only highlight the failings of the criminal justice system but also illustrate the human capacity to endure and effect change in the face of monumental challenges.

The in-depth exploration of wrongful conviction cases reveals that these incidents are much more than legal errors; they are profound human stories intertwining loss, hope, and renewal. The individuals at the heart of these stories, who have transformed their painful experiences into sources of hope, serve as powerful examples of human resilience and potential. Their journeys encourage us to take an active role in creating a more equitable and empathetic society.

This exploration of resilience in the face of injustice shapes the ongoing narrative of this chapter. It emphasizes the emotional impact of wrongful convictions, offering insights into how individuals navigate and heal from these profound injustices. The focus here is on understanding the emotional journey of exonerees and how their experiences can guide us in confronting and overcoming our own life challenges.

In telling these stories, the narrative embraces the full spectrum of experiences associated with wrongful convictions. It's a comprehensive look at the struggles and triumphs involved, highlighting the indomitable human spirit and the transformative power of overcoming adversity. This approach paints a vivid picture of the endurance required to not only survive but also to emerge stronger and more empowered from such experiences.

The stories of those wrongfully convicted offer significant insights into the essence of human resilience and endurance. Their experiences, marked by prolonged periods of injustice, showcase not only the strength required to withstand such trials but also the profound capacity for hope and determination. These stories serve as compelling examples of the power of the human spirit to overcome severe adversity and to seek justice against daunting odds.

The case of Kevin Bailey exemplifies the relentless pursuit of truth and justice. His lengthy incarceration and eventual release highlight the vital role of perseverance and hope in challenging wrongful convictions. Bailey's journey is a testament to the importance of maintaining self-worth and determination in the face of a system that may be slow to acknowledge its mistakes. His story, shared by many others in similar situations, underscores the need for tenacity in seeking justice.

These stories also emphasize the indispensable role of community support in the journey toward exoneration. The involvement of advocacy groups, alongside the unwavering support of family and friends, plays a crucial role in aiding individuals through their legal battles. The presence of a supportive network is not only a source of emotional strength but also a key factor in navigating the complex path to clearing one's name. It's a reminder that in the struggle for justice, the solidarity and support of others can be a pivotal force in turning the tide of adversity.

The development of psychological resilience in exonerees is a remarkable process, emerging because of their challenging experiences. This resilience is a crucial lesson for anyone encountering adversity, showcasing the ability of individuals to not only endure significant challenges but also emerge stronger from them. These stories emphasize the ongoing need for changes in the justice system, highlighting the resilience as not only a personal triumph but also as a driving force for systemic reform.

The transformation journey experienced by exonerees is a significant aspect of their stories. It involves a deep reevaluation and reconstruction of their identities, shaped not by the injustices they suffered but by their resilience and growth throughout their ordeal. This process of transformation showcases the profound capacity for self-renewal and the pursuit of dignity, offering insights into the strength and adaptability of the human spirit.

Moreover, the experiences of exonerees illuminate the importance of perseverance and the strength that can be found in embracing vulnerability. Their stories, far from being mere accounts of suffering, are powerful calls to action. They prompt a deeper examination of our societal structures and personal attitudes, urging us to recognize and address the systemic issues that lead to wrongful convictions. These narratives inspire a commitment to advocacy and change, both within us and in the world around us.

Delving further into the experiences of exonerees, we see their narratives as universally relatable, touching on the core of the human struggle against adversity. These stories, while rooted in the context of a flawed judicial system, offer broader insights into the human capacity for resilience and growth. They reflect a journey that many can empathize with, providing lessons in overcoming significant life challenges.

Each account of wrongful conviction, rich with perseverance and resilience, goes beyond mere struggle against injustice; they are powerful tales of redemption. These narratives of personal rebuilding and discovery of truths offer a mirror to the universal human experience of overcoming adversity. They underscore a shared quest for justice and a testament to the indomitable human spirit.

The shared path of exonerees illustrates a broader human saga, beginning with the jolt of facing injustice and culminating in the triumph of exoneration. This journey, marked by an unshakeable commitment to truth, unfolds as a series of inspiring steps, each showcasing the resilience and strength that characterize the human journey in the face of adversity.

Confronting both systemic imperfections and individual challenges, exonerees' newfound strength stands as a powerful symbol of human endurance and adaptability. These narratives reinforce the idea that our power lies in how we respond to life's unexpected turns. They illustrate a journey of redemption that encompasses more than legal vindication; it involves a profound journey of healing and personal narrative reclamation.

As we approach the conclusion of this chapter, we reach a moment of contemplation, not just about the content but about the broader themes of justice, identity, and self-discovery. This moment serves to recognize the bravery of exonerees and to resonate with the resilience present in each of us. It underscores the imperative to keep advocating for justice and to face adversity with a commitment to truth and integrity.

The resilience and transformation journey experienced by exonerees is a testament to human courage and our potential for growth. Their stories, more than just narratives of hardship, are beacons of hope and inspiration. They remind us that in our darkest times, there lies the potential for significant change and renewal, illuminating paths out of even the deepest shadows.

These stories, rich in lessons of perseverance and renewal, urge us to actively participate in shaping a more compassionate and just world. They encourage us not only to challenge injustices within our systems but also to uplift and support those in the struggle for truth and rectification. Embracing this call to action, we are inspired to embody the resilience and hope these narratives represent, propelling us forward in our individual journeys towards deeper understanding, personal growth, and empowerment.

Chapter Three
Finding Strength In The Struggle

In the intricate web of life, where the threads of adversity and strength are closely interwoven, our deepest challenges often emerge as the most profound sources of our personal growth and understanding. My journey, marked by an unjust system and a wrongful conviction, is not just a tale of personal strife but a narrative that resonates with anyone who has ever faced loss, grief, or isolation.

The awakening to a harsh reality, where one's freedom and dignity are stripped away, is a jolting experience that tests the human spirit. It's in these moments of despair that the essence of resilience is both challenged and nurtured. For me, this awakening was not just about confronting the flaws of the criminal justice system but also about facing the internal battles that such a crisis ignites.

My story, although unique in its details, shares the common themes of struggle and perseverance that echo in the lives of many. It's a journey that illustrates the resilience of the human spirit in the face of extreme hardship. The wrongful conviction was a crucible, an experience that, although unwanted, became the catalyst for a deeper understanding of myself and the world.

The initial shock of my wrongful conviction was like being thrust into a relentless storm. As the reality of my situation sunk in, I was engulfed by a whirlwind of emotions—anger, disbelief, and a profound sense of injustice. But amidst this turmoil, a spark of resilience began to flicker. It was this resilience that sustained me, that transformed my struggle into a source of strength and advocacy.

As I navigated the complexities of the legal system, I became acutely aware of its imperfections. The experience illuminated not just the personal impact of wrongful convictions but also their broader societal implications. It became clear that my story was part of a larger narrative, one that included countless others who had been wrongfully accused and whose voices were yet to be heard.

In this journey, I discovered that true strength is not just about enduring hardship but about transforming it into an opportunity for growth and advocacy. It's about using one's experiences to shed light on systemic issues and to inspire change. This transformation was not immediate; it was a gradual process that required introspection, determination, and an unwavering commitment to justice and truth.

As the narrative of my life unfolded in the shadow of wrongful conviction, it became a testament to the power of human endurance and the capacity for change. This phase of my life was not merely about survival; it was an awakening to the profound inequities and hidden strengths within myself and society. My struggle, while deeply personal, was also a mirror reflecting the struggles of many who grapple with injustice in its myriad forms.

In the depths of my despair, I found a wellspring of resilience. This resilience was not born out of naivety or blind optimism, but from a hard-fought battle with reality. It was a resilience forged in the crucible of injustice, fueled by the desire for truth and a longing for justice not only for me but for others who had fallen prey to a flawed system.

This journey illuminated the interconnectedness of our struggles. My fight became a shared battle, a unifying cry against the systemic failures that plague our justice system. I learned that my voice, once silenced and discounted, had the power to resonate with others, to mobilize action and inspire change.

Amidst the turmoil, there emerged a profound sense of purpose. This purpose transcended the confines of my personal ordeal, reaching into the hearts and minds of others. It became a driving force, propelling me to use my experience as a platform to advocate for systemic change and to offer hope to those who felt voiceless and forgotten.

The lessons learned were manifold. The most striking was the realization that our greatest trials often unveil our most significant strengths. In the face of adversity, we discover aspects of our character that remain hidden in times of comfort. These discoveries are not just revelations of personal fortitude but also beacons of hope for others traversing similar paths.

My journey through the labyrinth of the criminal justice system also shed light on the importance of empathy and understanding. I learned that the path to healing and redemption is paved with the compassion we extend to ourselves and others. This empathy is not a mere sentiment; it's a powerful tool that breaks down barriers and fosters a deeper connection with the human experience.

As my story unfolded, it became clear that the scars of wrongful conviction were also marks of transformation. These scars told a story of pain, yes, but also of triumph, of a spirit that refused to be broken by the weight of injustice. They became symbols of my resilience, testaments to the indomitable nature of the human will.

In the heart of this transformative journey, I found solace and strength in the shared experiences of others. Connecting with fellow exonerees, hearing their stories of injustice and resilience, created a sense of community and solidarity that was both healing and empowering. These connections served as a stark reminder that my struggle was part of a larger narrative, a collective call for justice and reform.

The path of advocacy and reform was illuminated by these shared experiences. Each story of wrongful conviction highlighted not only the individual pain and resilience but also the systemic flaws that needed addressing. It became evident that real change required a multifaceted approach, one that involved not just legal reforms but also a shift in societal attitudes and awareness.

My engagement in advocacy work led to deeper insights into the complexities of the criminal justice system. It was a system fraught with biases, procedural inefficiencies, and a lack of accountability that often resulted in tragic miscarriages of justice. This understanding fueled my commitment to fight for reforms that would ensure fairness and prevent future wrongful convictions.

This fight for justice was not a solitary endeavor. It was bolstered by the support of legal professionals, activists, and communities who shared the vision of a more equitable justice system. Collaborating with these allies, leveraging their expertise and resources, amplified the impact of our collective efforts. It is a powerful demonstration of how unity and collaboration can bring about significant societal changes.

The journey also taught me the value of patience and persistence. Change, especially at the systemic level, is seldom immediate. It requires continuous effort, unwavering dedication, and the resilience to face setbacks and challenges. This perseverance was a testament to the belief that even the most entrenched systems could be reformed with sustained effort and collective action.

As I continued to navigate the intricacies of advocacy and reform, I also delved into understanding the human psyche in the face of adversity. The wrongful conviction experience, while unique, shared common emotional and psychological elements with other life challenges. It was a profound study in human resilience, showcasing how individuals can find strength and hope in the most despairing circumstances.

Through this journey, I learned the importance of self-care and mental health. Coping with the stress and trauma of wrongful conviction required not just external support but also internal healing. It was essential to recognize and address the emotional and psychological impact of my experience, to seek therapy and counseling when needed, and to develop healthy coping mechanisms.

This phase of my journey was not just about confronting external challenges; it was a deep dive into self-reflection and personal growth. The resilience I had cultivated was not only a shield against the hardships of wrongful conviction but also a tool for introspection and self-improvement. This period became an opportunity to reassess my values, goals, and the very essence of my identity.

The process of rebuilding my life post-exoneration was akin to piecing together a puzzle. Each piece represented a different aspect of my life – professional aspirations, personal relationships, societal roles. The challenge was not just in finding where these pieces fit but in reimagining and reshaping them to create a new, coherent whole. This task required creativity, flexibility, and a willingness to venture into uncharted territories.

In this rebuilding process, I learned the significance of fostering positive relationships and building a supportive network. The bonds formed with family, friends, and fellow advocates provided a foundation of support that was crucial for my reintegration into society. These relationships were not just a source of comfort; they were instrumental in my journey towards healing and growth.

The path to recovery also highlighted the importance of giving back to the community. Using my experiences to help others became a source of fulfillment and purpose. Whether it was mentoring young people, speaking at events, or participating in advocacy efforts, each act of service was a step towards not only personal healing but also contributing to a greater good.

As I embarked on this path of service and advocacy, I was struck by the power of storytelling. Sharing my story, and hearing those of others, was not just cathartic; it was a powerful tool for raising awareness and inspiring change. These stories, raw and authentic, had the power to move hearts and minds, bridging the gap between personal experiences and broader social issues.

The struggle against a flawed justice system is not a solitary battle. It's shared by many who have endured the harrowing journey of wrongful convictions. Their stories are not just tales of injustice but also powerful examples of resilience and hope. Consider the case of Christopher Tapp, who served 21 years for a crime he did not commit. His eventual exoneration came after a long battle, marked by unwavering determination and the support of those who believed in his innocence.

Like my own experience, Christopher's story is a poignant reminder of the fallibility of the justice system and the resilience of the human spirit. His journey, like mine, underscores the importance of persistence in the face of adversity. It's a testament to the fact that the path to justice, though fraught with obstacles, can lead to vindication and change.

Another compelling story is that of Malcolm Alexander, who spent 38 years in prison for a wrongful conviction. Malcolm's exoneration was a result of new DNA evidence, highlighting the critical role of scientific advancements in uncovering the truth. His story is not just about the years lost but about the strength and courage to rebuild life from the ashes of injustice.

These stories resonate deeply with me, reinforcing the belief that wrongful convictions are not isolated incidents but a systemic issue that demands attention and action. They also serve as powerful reminders of the capacity for growth and transformation in the face of unimaginable challenges.

Let us delve deeper into the psychological impact of wrongful convictions, not only on the individuals directly affected but also on their families and communities. The emotional toll of these experiences often extends far beyond the exonerees, affecting the lives of many around them. The chapter explores the ripple effects of these traumas and the importance of a supportive network in the healing process.

It is imperative we highlight the critical role of advocacy groups and legal reforms in addressing the issue of wrongful convictions. The work of organizations like the The Innocence Center, and the Innocence Project, which has helped free numerous innocent people from prison, is vital in this fight for justice. Their efforts not only bring individual cases to light but also contribute to systemic changes that can prevent future injustices.

As this book progresses, I'll continue to weave together personal narratives, real-life cases, and broader discussions on systemic reforms and mental health, aiming to create a compelling, informative, and thought provoking narrative that will resonate with you all.

As we draw Chapter 3 to a close, the story of resilience in the face of wrongful convictions converge with a universal message of hope and inner freedom. The stories I've shared here, from Christopher Tapp's two-decade fight for freedom to Malcolm Alexander's perseverance through 38 years of wrongful imprisonment, exemplify not only the grave costs of a flawed justice system but also the indomitable spirit that prevails in the darkest of times.

The personal odysseys of these individuals, set against the backdrop of systemic reform and advocacy, resonate with the broader human quest for dignity and truth. Their battles, though deeply personal, reflect a collective struggle for a fair and just society. It is within these stories that we find a roadmap for our own journeys, a guide to navigating the complexities of hardship and the pathways to inner freedom.

Embracing the lessons from these journeys encourages us to look inward, to find resilience within ourselves, and to discover that true freedom often begins in the confines of our own minds. The chains of injustice, while they may bind the body, need not restrain the spirit. Inner freedom is a state of being that transcends physical limitations, allowing us to remain undeterred by the confines of our circumstances.

In this chapter, we have traversed the landscape of wrongful convictions and witnessed the transformative power of hope and human resilience. We have seen that redemption is more than a legal exoneration; it is a rebirth of self, a reclaiming of one's narrative, and a restoration of one's place in the world. This redemption is not only for those who have been wrongfully convicted but for anyone who has faced the confines of misfortune and injustice.

As we move forward, let us carry with us the understanding that our spirit need not be confined by the walls built by others or by the circumstances in which we find ourselves. Inner freedom is achieved through the relentless pursuit of truth, the courage to face our challenges, and the empathy we extend to ourselves and to those around us. It is fostered by the communities we build, the relationships we cherish, and the causes for which we stand.

The conclusion of this chapter is not the end of the conversation but an invitation to continue the journey toward justice and self-discovery. It is a call to recognize the resilience within each of us and to work towards creating systems that reflect our highest values of fairness, compassion, and equity.

As we turn the page, we prepare to delve into the next chapter: "Inner Freedom Amongst Confinement," where we will explore the internal landscapes of freedom and the ways in which we can cultivate peace and strength, regardless of our external environments. The stories of the wrongfully convicted have much to teach us about this inner sanctuary, providing inspiration for all who seek liberation from the confines of adversity.

Chapter Four
Inner Freedom Amongst Confinement

In the quiet corners of our minds lies a realm of immeasurable depth, a space where true freedom resides. This chapter delves into the exploration of this inner freedom, a journey that transcends physical boundaries and external constraints. It's a venture into the heart of our being, uncovering the boundless potential that lies within.

The pursuit of inner freedom begins with the acknowledgment that our mental and emotional landscapes are ours to navigate. Despite the limitations imposed by our external circumstances, within us is an unconfined space where thoughts and emotions can roam freely. This realization empowers us to take control of our inner narrative, to craft a story of resilience and strength, regardless of the physical confines we might face.

Throughout this voyage of self-discovery, we confront various facets of our inner selves – fears, hopes, dreams, and doubts. It's a process of introspection and self-discovery, where we come face-to-face with our vulnerabilities and learn to embrace them as integral parts of our identity. This path isn't devoid of challenges; it requires us to confront uncomfortable truths, to question long-held beliefs, and to reassess our values.

In the heart of Los Angeles California, a bustling city where the future seemed woven into the very fabric of the streets, there lived a young woman named Maya. She reflected contemporary success, with a prestigious job at a tech firm, a sleek apartment, and a social media profile curated to perfection. Yet, beneath this veneer of accomplishment, Maya felt a gnawing emptiness, a dissonance between her external world and her inner life.

Every day, Maya commuted through the crowded streets, her thoughts lost in the podcasts and audiobooks that spoke of self-improvement and success. Her life was a meticulously planned routine, from morning workouts to late-night work emails. But one evening, as she worked overtime in her cubicle, a seemingly mundane incident set a new course for her life. Maya discovered an old, forgotten journal tucked away in her drawer, left by a previous occupant of her workspace. It was filled with reflections and musings about finding meaning and happiness in life, written by someone who seemed to have struggled with the same sense of confinement Maya felt.

Intrigued and unexpectedly moved, Maya began to read the journal during her lunch breaks. The anonymous writer talked about the courage to seek one's own path, to question the relentless pursuit of material success, and to find richness in simplicity and authentic connections. This journal became Maya's secret escape, a window to a different perspective that she hadn't dared to consider in her own life.

As days turned into weeks, the words from the journal started to echo in Maya's thoughts. She began to question the relentless pace of her life, the endless chase for promotions and recognition, and the superficial connections that formed her social circle. The more she reflected, the more Maya realized how much of her life was lived according to others' expectations and societal norms, rather than her own values and desires.

This inner turmoil reached its peak one cold winter night, as Maya lay awake, the city's lights casting shadows across her room. In that quiet hour, she made a decision that felt both terrifying and exhilarating. She decided to step away from her current life, to embark on a journey of self-discovery, not to distant lands or mythical places, but within the very city she lived in, and within herself.

Maya started by taking a sabbatical from work, a decision that shocked her colleagues and friends. She began exploring parts of the city she had never seen before, from quaint neighborhoods with history-laden streets to serene parks where the city's noise faded into a distant hum. She volunteered at local community centers, connected with people from walks of life vastly different from her own, and started attending workshops and talks on topics ranging from philosophy to sustainable living.

Each new experience was a thread in the tapestry of her transformation. Maya learned to embrace simplicity, finding joy in moments like reading a book in a sunlit cafe or having heartfelt conversations with strangers who soon

34

became friends. She discovered a passion for writing, channeling her journey into words that she shared on a blog, resonating with others who felt trapped in their own invisible cages.

But the journey was not without its struggles. There were moments of doubt, loneliness, and fear. Maya often found herself questioning her choices, especially as she saw her peers advancing in their careers and personal lives. However, these challenges only deepened her resolve, helping her understand that true empowerment and freedom were not about external achievements, but about inner peace and living authentically.

As months passed, Maya's journey became a story of transformation, not just for herself but for others who followed her journey through her writings. She returned to her job not with a sense of resignation, but with a new perspective, integrating her newfound values into her work and relationships. She became a voice in her community, advocating for mental well-being, work-life balance, and the courage to define one's own path.

Maya's story is a testament to the possibility of finding inner freedom amidst mental confinement. It is a narrative not of escape, but of engagement with the world in a more meaningful and authentic way. Through her experiences, she uncovered the hidden gems of wisdom that lay not in distant, mythical places, but within the complexities and simplicities of everyday life. Her journey from injustice to empowerment was a journey of awakening to the beauty of living a life true to oneself.

In this exploration, we find that inner freedom is about more than just the absence of physical constraints – it's about the liberation of the spirit. It's about finding peace and contentment within us, regardless of our external environment. This form of freedom is cultivated through practices such as mindfulness, meditation, and creative expression. Activities that allow us to connect deeply with our inner selves and to express our true nature.

Through these practices, we begin to understand that inner freedom is intrinsically linked to resilience. It's about developing the mental and emotional fortitude to withstand life's trials and tribulations. This resilience is not a static trait but a dynamic process, evolving with each challenge we face and each obstacle we overcome.

Hope and optimism serve as vital companions on this transformative journey. These forces are not mere feelings but essential energies that fuel our progress. They are the lenses through which we view even the most challenging situations with a sense of possibility and positivity. Hope and optimism keep our spirits buoyant, reminding us that there is always light, even in the darkest of places.

While the journey is deeply personal, it is not solitary. Our connections with others provide support, understanding, and a sense of belonging, all of which are essential for nurturing our inner worlds. These relationships remind us that even in confinement, we are not alone. We are part of a larger human story, connected by our shared experiences and emotions.

As we delve into the nuances of inner freedom, we enter the realm of emotional intelligence – the ability to understand and manage our emotions effectively. Emotional intelligence becomes a cornerstone in building inner freedom, as it enables us to navigate our feelings with clarity and purpose. It's about recognizing our emotional responses, understanding their origins, and learning how to channel them in ways that are constructive rather than destructive.

This development of emotional intelligence leads us to a deeper understanding of empathy. The ability to connect with and understand the emotions of others. Empathy enriches our inner lives, enabling us to forge deeper connections and to appreciate the complex tapestry of human experience. It's not merely about feeling what others feel, but about using that understanding to foster compassion and connection.

Inner freedom also involves the cultivation of resilience. This resilience is not just the ability to bounce back from adversity but to grow and thrive because of it. It's about seeing challenges as opportunities for personal development, about learning from every experience, and about using those lessons to become stronger, wiser, and more adaptable.

Understanding the concept of purpose is vital – it involves grasping what drives us, what gives our lives meaning, and how we can align our actions with our deepest values. Finding purpose in our lives, whether in grand ambitions or small daily actions, becomes a powerful motivator and a source of fulfillment and satisfaction.

During this journey, you will encounter moments of profound realization. Moments where you come to understand something essential about yourself or the world around you. These realizations often come unexpectedly, in moments of quiet reflection or during challenging experiences, offering glimpses into the depths of your own being.

Navigating this path of inner discovery requires recognizing the importance of adaptability. The ability to adjust your thoughts, emotions, and actions in response to changing circumstances. Adaptability is a key aspect of inner freedom, allowing you to remain fluid and flexible in the face of life's uncertainties.

To actively cultivate a mindset that nurtures this state, you must begin by acknowledging the power of your thoughts. Your thoughts are the seeds that grow into the reality of your life. Just as a garden requires careful tending, so too do your minds need attention and care. By planting positive, empowering thoughts, and diligently weeding out negative ones, you shape your inner world and, consequently, your external experiences.

This mindful cultivation of thoughts leads to the development of a strong, purposeful character. You become what you think. By consistently directing your thoughts towards your goals and values, you mold your character to align with your aspirations. This process is not about repression but about choosing thoughts that serve you, thoughts that are in harmony with your true selves.

The journey to inner freedom is also about understanding the link between your thoughts and your circumstances. Often, you perceive yourselves as victims of your circumstances, but your thoughts, actions, and habits create the conditions of your lives. By acknowledging this, you empower yourselves to change your circumstances through the transformation of your thoughts.

This transformation requires purposeful thinking. Without a clear purpose, your thoughts can wander aimlessly, leading to a lack of achievement and fulfillment. By focusing your thoughts on a specific purpose, you give direction to your efforts and infuse your actions with meaning.

Overcoming doubts and fears is paramount. These negative thoughts are the greatest barriers to achievement and success. By conquering these limiting beliefs, you open the door to a world of possibilities. Difficulties and challenges are not roadblocks but opportunities for growth and learning.

In this context, serenity becomes an asset. A calm, peaceful mind is not only a source of strength but also a reflection of wisdom. Cultivating tranquility amidst life's storms enables you to respond to situations with clarity and poise. This tranquility is not passivity but a dynamic state of being, allowing you to interact with the world with balance and grace.

To nurture a mindset conducive to inner freedom, it's crucial to start by acknowledging the immense power of your thoughts. Your thoughts are not just fleeting mental images; they are the architects of your reality. If you allow negative, self-defeating thoughts to take root, they shape your lives in ways that limit your potential. On the other hand, when you consciously cultivate positive, empowering thoughts, you lay the foundation for a life filled with growth, resilience, and freedom.

But how do you transform your thought patterns? It begins with self-awareness. You must become vigilant observers of your thoughts, recognizing patterns that lead you astray and actively replacing them with thoughts that align with your true aspirations. This is not a one-time effort but a continuous process of mental gardening. Every day, you need to weed out negativity and plant seeds of positivity.

A practical way to start is through daily affirmations and visualization. Affirmations are positive statements that can help to challenge and overcome self-sabotaging and negative thoughts. When you repeatedly affirm your strengths and goals, you start to rewire your brain to believe in your capability to achieve them. Visualization, on the other hand, involves creating a mental image of achieving your goals. It's a powerful tool that primes your mind and body to act in ways that align with your visualized objectives.

Furthermore, developing emotional intelligence is key to navigating the complexities of your inner world. Emotional intelligence involves understanding and managing your emotions effectively. It's about recognizing your emotional triggers, understanding why they occur, and learning how to respond to them in healthy ways. By developing emotional intelligence, you gain control over your reactions, making you more resilient in the face of adversity.

To enhance emotional intelligence, start by practicing mindfulness. Mindfulness is the quality of being fully present and engaged with whatever you're doing now — free from distraction or judgment, and aware of your thoughts and feelings without getting caught up in them. By cultivating mindfulness through practices like meditation, you can observe your emotions without being overwhelmed by them, allowing you to respond rather than react.

Now, as you prepare to conclude this chapter, reflect on the importance of this journey into the depths of inner freedom. It is a journey that commences within you, unfolding in the recesses of your mind and heart. It is a voyage that extends beyond the confines of your physical existence, transcending the boundaries of time and space. It is a quest for self-discovery, resilience, and limitless potential.

In the chapters that follow, we will continue to explore the profound realms of the human spirit, the pursuit of justice, and the transformative power of forgiveness. We will delve into the significance of chasing dreams, the profound impact of pain and empowerment, and the enduring value of resilience and hope.

This journey is not just about finding strength in adversity; it is about unearthing the depths of your potential, the vastness of your influence, and the limitless possibilities that reside within you. It is a journey that challenges you to evolve, to grow, and to emerge stronger, wiser, and more empowered than ever before.

Embrace it with an open heart, for the adventure has just begun. Your destiny is in your hands, and the world awaits the remarkable story that only you can tell. As you move forward, may your spirit soar, may your heart be filled with hope, and may your path be illuminated by the radiant light of your own inner freedom.

In the tapestry of existence, your journey is a thread of resilience, a thread of hope, a thread of boundless possibility. It is a voyage into the very core of your being, a quest for a life defined not by limitations, but by the expanse of your inner freedom. The chapters ahead hold the promise of profound discoveries, inspiring revelations, and transformative insights. Open your heart and mind to the wondrous odyssey that lies ahead, for within you, the journey continues.

Chapter Five
The Journey to Justice

Justice – a concept revered and sought after, yet often elusive and complex. My journey towards justice, a path entwined with challenges and revelations, serves as a microcosm of a larger quest – a quest for fairness, truth, and the upholding of rights within a flawed and often bewildering legal system.

This chapter delves into the core discoveries that have shaped my understanding of justice, resilience, and personal growth. As I embarked on this transformative journey, I unearthed profound insights that extend far beyond the realm of the legal system. These discoveries have become guiding principles, offering solace and wisdom to those who have faced extreme hardship, loss, grievances, or isolation.

The first revelation emerged from the crucible of advocacy. As I confronted a legal system that at times seemed indifferent to the truth, I discovered the transformative power of raising one's voice. Advocacy, in its essence, is not confined to legal battles alone. It represents a universal tool for change, capable of challenging injustices and sparking reform in various domains of life.

Advocacy, I realized, is not solely about speaking out; it is about giving voice to the voiceless, shedding light on the darkest corners of society, and demanding accountability from those in power. It is a force that empowers individuals to become agents of change, weaving threads of resilience and determination into the fabric of society.

Advocacy is not a solitary endeavor; it thrives on collective action. It is a call to unite, to stand alongside others who share a common vision of justice, and to amplify each other's voices. In this unity, we find strength, solidarity, and the potential to dismantle systemic barriers that perpetuate injustice.

The second revelation stemmed from the crucible of self-discovery. As I navigated the labyrinthine complexities of the legal system, I embarked on a parallel journey into the depths of my own being. Adversity, I discovered, has a unique capacity to unearth hidden reservoirs of strength and resilience.

In the face of seemingly insurmountable odds, I confronted my deepest fears and insecurities. I questioned long-held beliefs about right and wrong, and I examined my role within the larger societal context. This introspection was not limited to my personal circumstances; it extended to the broader implications of my fight for justice.

Self-discovery, I found, is a dynamic process. It requires the courage to delve into the recesses of one's own psyche, to confront the scars of the past, and to emerge with a deeper understanding of one's values and purpose. In this process, I discovered that our individual journeys are interconnected with the broader tapestry of human experience.

The third revelation was forged through unwavering perseverance. The wheels of justice often turn slowly, testing the limits of patience and resolve. It is in these moments of despair and uncertainty that the true test of resilience arises.

Perseverance, I realized, is not a passive endurance of hardships, but an active force that propels us forward. It is the determination to continue the fight, even when the path is obscured by shadows. It is a testament to the human spirit's capacity for endurance and its unwavering pursuit of what is right and fair.

Throughout my journey, I found that perseverance in the face of adversity is a potent tool. It keeps the flames of hope and justice burning, even in the darkest of times. It is a testament to the indomitable human spirit, capable of surmounting the most formidable obstacles.

These three discoveries have become guiding beacons, illuminating the path towards justice, resilience, and personal growth. They transcend the confines of the legal system, offering insights that resonate with those who have faced extreme hardship and adversity. As we move forward, may these discoveries serve as sources of strength and inspiration, guiding us on our individual journeys towards justice and inner transformation.

So, how can these discoveries be acquired, obtained, learned, practiced, and ultimately mastered by anyone who has faced extreme hardship, loss, grievances, or isolation? These are not elusive secrets but rather guiding principles accessible to all who embark on the path of self-discovery and transformation.

Advocacy is not a skill reserved for the legal elite; it is a potent force that can be harnessed by anyone willing to champion a cause. To acquire the art of advocacy, one must first find a cause that resonates deeply with their values and beliefs. It might be a personal experience of injustice, a social issue that ignites their passion, or a community in need of support.

Next comes the process of education. Just as I immersed myself in understanding the intricacies of the legal system, individuals can dedicate themselves to learning about the issues they wish to advocate for. This involves research, seeking out reputable sources, and staying informed about the latest developments in the field.

The practice of advocacy requires finding one's voice, which often begins with sharing personal stories and experiences. Writing, speaking, or engaging in community discussions are all ways to start. Building alliances with like-minded individuals and organizations amplifies the impact of advocacy, and these connections can be formed through networking and active involvement in relevant communities.

Ultimately, mastery of advocacy comes from a continuous commitment to the cause. It is the willingness to persevere, even when faced with obstacles or setbacks. As individuals persist in advocating for what they believe is just and right, they not only create change in their chosen field but also cultivate their own resilience and sense of purpose.

The journey of self-discovery often begins with a moment of reckoning, a recognition that life's challenges have the potential to transform us. To embark on this path, individuals can start by acknowledging their own vulnerabilities and past traumas. This act of introspection opens the door to self-awareness and growth.

Self-discovery is nurtured through the practice of mindfulness. This involves paying close attention to one's thoughts, emotions, and reactions. Journaling, meditation, or seeking guidance from a mental health professional can all aid in this process. It is through mindfulness that we unearth our hidden reservoirs of strength and resilience.

As individuals delve deeper into self-discovery, they should explore their values, beliefs, and life purpose. What matters most to them? What drives them to overcome adversity? These questions provide a compass for navigating life's challenges and finding meaning during hardship.

Ultimately, self-discovery is an ongoing journey. It is about evolving and growing as individuals. It requires patience and self-compassion, as well as a willingness to confront discomfort and uncertainty. By embracing these principles, individuals can find their own paths to resilience and personal growth.

Perseverance, the unwavering commitment to a cause or goal, is a quality that can be cultivated over time. It starts with setting clear intentions and defining what one hopes to achieve. Whether it's seeking justice, personal healing, or societal change, having a clear vision provides a sense of purpose.

To master perseverance, individuals must be prepared for challenges and setbacks. They should understand that the path to any significant goal is rarely linear. When obstacles arise, it's important to view them as opportunities for growth rather than insurmountable barriers.

A support system is invaluable on the journey of perseverance. Just as I leaned on lawyers, activists, family, and friends, individuals should seek out allies who share their vision and can provide encouragement and guidance. These relationships bolster one's resilience in the face of adversity.

Finally, mastering perseverance involves a deep commitment to one's values and beliefs. It means staying true to one's principles even when the going gets tough. This unwavering dedication, combined with a willingness to adapt and learn from failures, is the essence of resilience.

In essence, these three discoveries are not exclusive to my journey alone. They are universal principles that anyone can embrace and integrate into their lives. Advocacy, self-discovery, and perseverance are not mere concepts; they are transformative tools that empower individuals to navigate the complexities of life, find their voices, and become beacons of resilience and justice.

In my own journey, as a wrongfully convicted individual who navigated the labyrinthine corridors of the justice system, I discovered that the lessons I learned hold relevance not only for those entangled in legal battles but for every person facing life's trials and tribulations.

My experience of advocacy, born out of necessity, serves as a testament to the transformative power of standing up for what one believes in. It's a reminder that we all possess the capacity to advocate for ourselves and for others in times of need. Whether we're seeking justice in a courtroom, confronting an unjust situation at work, or advocating for a loved one, the principles remain the same. We must educate ourselves, find our voices, and persist in the face of adversity.

Self-discovery through adversity is a journey I embarked upon out of sheer survival instinct. It's a journey that reveals the profound strength and resilience that reside within each of us. When faced with hardships, we have a choice – to succumb or to rise. The key to self-discovery is to confront our vulnerabilities, embrace our imperfections, and understand that adversity is not a mark of weakness but a catalyst for growth. By practicing mindfulness, reflecting on our values, and seeking meaning in our struggles, we can emerge from adversity stronger and wiser.

The resilience of perseverance, cultivated during my years of wrongful incarceration, is a lesson that resonates universally. Life often throws curveballs, and our ability to persist in the face of adversity is a measure of our character. Whether we're striving for personal goals, pursuing justice, or simply navigating the ups and downs of life, resilience is our greatest asset. It involves setting clear intentions, expecting setbacks, leaning on a support system, and unwaveringly adhering to our values.

Now, as we draw this chapter to a close, it is my hope that these discoveries, born from my journey through the shadows of injustice, resonate deeply with you. While my story may be one of wrongful conviction, the principles of advocacy, self-discovery, and perseverance are threads that weave through the tapestry of human experience.

As you reflect on the trials and tribulations you may face in your own life, remember that you, too, have the power to advocate for change, to embark on a journey of self-discovery, and to cultivate the resilience of perseverance. Whether you find yourself in a courtroom, a challenging relationship, a career crossroads, or simply amid life's uncertainties, these principles can guide you.

It is my belief that the journey to justice, resilience, and personal growth is not limited to those who have faced wrongful convictions or legal battles. It is a journey that each of us can embark upon, no matter the circumstances. In the chapters that follow, we will delve deeper into the practical applications of these principles, drawing inspiration from real-life stories and experiences that exemplify their transformative power.

For now, I invite you to contemplate how these discoveries can find a place in your own life's narrative. In the quest for justice, resilience, and personal growth, we are not alone. We are united by our shared humanity, our capacity for advocacy, our potential for self-discovery, and our unwavering resilience in the face of adversity.

As we move forward, let us carry with us the lessons learned from my journey and the journeys of countless others who have faced hardship and emerged stronger. Together, we can illuminate the path to justice and resilience, not only within the flawed corridors of the justice system but in every corner of our lives.

Chapter Six
Reconstructing Life After Loss

The experience of life is often marked by periods of rebuilding, of picking up the pieces after unexpected losses and charting a new course forward. For me, the challenge was not just in the rebuilding but in what was lost – time, opportunities, dreams – all taken by a wrongful conviction that altered the trajectory of my life.

Reconstructing life after such a profound loss is an experience that transcends the physical act of rebuilding. It's an exploration into the depths of one's soul, a quest to rediscover identity, purpose, and meaning in a world that has been irrevocably changed. It's a path of healing, of growth, and ultimately, of transformation.

The first step in this reconstruction is the process of grieving. Grieving is not just an expression of sorrow for what has been lost; it is an acknowledgement of the impact of that loss on our lives. It is a necessary and healthy response, a way of honoring the significance of what we have endured and giving ourselves permission to feel the full range of emotions that come with it.

Grieving, in my experience, was a journey in itself – a journey through stages of denial, anger, bargaining, depression, and acceptance. Each stage brought its own challenges and insights, but they all shared a common purpose: to help me come to terms with my past and to pave the way for a future.

Acceptance, the final stage of grieving, was perhaps the most transformative. It was not about resigning myself to my fate but about acknowledging the reality of my situation and recognizing that, despite the injustices I had faced, I still had the power to shape my future. Acceptance was a turning point, a moment of clarity that shifted my focus from what I had lost to what I could still gain.

This shift marked the beginning of the rebuilding process. Rebuilding after a loss as significant as wrongful imprisonment is not just about restoring what was lost; it's about creating something new, something that reflects the person you have become through your trials. It is a process of redefining goals, reassessing values, and reimagining possibilities.

One of the first steps in this rebuilding process was reestablishing connections with family and friends. These relationships, which had been strained and tested during my time in prison, were essential to my healing and recovery. They provided a support system, a network of love and understanding that was crucial in helping me navigate the complexities of reentering society.

Reconnecting with loved ones also meant rebuilding trust, both in myself and in others. Trust that had been eroded by years of injustice and isolation needed to be nurtured and restored. It was a gradual process, one that required patience, openness, and a willingness to be vulnerable.

As I worked to rebuild relationships, I also focused on rebuilding my career and professional life. This involved identifying new goals and aspirations, assessing my skills and interests, and finding ways to translate my experiences into meaningful work. It was about taking the lessons learned from my ordeal and using them to create a career that was not just about making a living but about making a difference.

This career reconstruction was not without its challenges. The stigma of a criminal record, even one that had been overturned, was a barrier that needed to be overcome. It required resilience, determination, and a proactive approach to creating opportunities where they seemed scarce.

Beyond the professional realm, rebuilding also involved addressing the emotional and psychological scars left by my experiences. This involved seeking therapy, engaging in self-care practices, and developing coping strategies to deal with the lingering effects of trauma. It was about giving myself the time and space to heal, to process my experiences, and to emerge stronger and more self-aware.

As part of this emotional and psychological rebuilding, I focused on cultivating a mindset of growth and positivity. This involved challenging negative thought patterns, practicing gratitude, and embracing a perspective that viewed challenges as opportunities for growth. It was a mindset that empowered me to see beyond the limitations of my past and to envision a future filled with potential.

The road to reconstructing life after loss also involves embracing a unique perspective on forgiveness. For me, forgiveness was not about seeking to absolve those who wronged me or wrestling with the notion of whether I could ever truly forgive them. It was about recognizing that holding onto anger, resentment, and bitterness would only prolong my own suffering and allow the past to maintain an unhealthy grip on my life.

In my journey, forgiveness meant taking a different approach. It involved acknowledging that no matter how much I dwelled on the injustices I had endured, it wouldn't change the past. What had happened to me was a painful reality that I couldn't alter. Brian's personal take on forgiveness is grounded in the belief that no one, and no experience, deserves the power to dictate the course of your life. It's about regaining control over your own narrative and not letting the shadows of the past cast darkness on your future.

This perspective allowed me to break free from the emotional chains that had bound me for so long. It was a process of releasing the grip of the past and choosing to move forward with my life. It was an act of self-empowerment, a declaration that I would not let the actions of others define my future.

Forgiveness, in this sense, became an act of self-compassion. It was an acknowledgment that I, too, had been affected by my experiences, that I had made mistakes and faced challenges along the way. It was about showing myself the same kindness, care, and understanding that I offered to others.

In the process of reconstruction, forgiveness became a cornerstone of my healing. It allowed me to reclaim my sense of self-worth and dignity. It allowed me to rebuild relationships with a foundation of trust and compassion. It allowed me to redirect my energy towards positive endeavors, rather than dwelling on the past.

As I continued to navigate the complexities of life after loss, I found solace in pursuing the dreams and aspirations that had been deferred by my wrongful conviction. These dreams, which had once seemed out of reach, became sources of inspiration and motivation.

The pursuit of deferred dreams was not without its challenges. It required determination, resilience, and the willingness to step outside my comfort zone. It meant facing uncertainty and taking risks, all while knowing that failure was a possibility. Yet, it was through this pursuit that I discovered the depth of my own potential.

Rebuilding life after loss is not a linear process; it is filled with setbacks and obstacles. It is a journey of highs and lows, of triumphs and disappointments. But it is also a journey of continuous growth and transformation.

Throughout this journey, I have come to understand the profound resilience that resides within each of us. It is a resilience that allows us to weather the storms of life, to adapt to new circumstances, and to emerge stronger than before. It is a resilience that reminds us of our inherent capacity to overcome adversity and find meaning in our experiences.

As I reflect on the path of reconstructing life after loss, I am reminded of the importance of hope. Hope is the guiding light that illuminates the darkest moments of our lives. It is the belief that better days are ahead, that we can rise above our challenges, and that our struggles have the potential to lead us to a brighter future.

In the chapters to come, we will delve deeper into the intricacies of this journey. We will explore the resilience that sustains us through each step, the transformative power of forgiveness, and the pursuit of dreams that have been deferred. We will also examine the importance of becoming a voice for change, the transformation of pain into empowerment, and the enduring hope that leads us forward.

Reconstructing life after loss is not just about rebuilding what was lost; it is about creating a life that is richer, more meaningful, and aligned with our true selves. It is a testament to the indomitable human spirit, a reminder that, even in the face of profound challenges, we have the capacity to thrive and find purpose in our journey.

Now, as we continue forward, let us do so with a sense of resilience, forgiveness, and hope. Let us embrace the opportunities for growth and transformation that lie ahead and let us carry with us the lessons learned from the journey of reconstruction.

In our journey of reconstructing life after loss, we've encountered the profound power of forgiveness. It's a power that liberates us from the chains of anger and bitterness, reminding us that we have the choice to release ourselves from the burden of carrying another's actions as our own.

The pursuit of deferred dreams has illuminated our path, reminding us that even in the wake of wrongful convictions and lost time, our aspirations remain within reach. Our dreams, once obscured by the shadows of injustice, have emerged as guiding stars, beckoning us towards a future filled with purpose and determination.

Rebuilding life after loss is a journey of rediscovery – of identity, purpose, and meaning. It necessitates the reestablishment of connections with loved ones, the rebuilding of trust, and the pursuit of new professional horizons. Through it all, we've uncovered the resilience that resides within us, propelling us forward, even in the face of seemingly insurmountable challenges.

Amidst the twists and turns of reconstruction, hope has remained our steadfast companion. It's the light that pierces the darkness, reminding us that even in our darkest moments, a brighter future awaits. It's the belief that our struggles are not in vain, but rather steppingstones on the path to a more meaningful existence.

As we reflect on the journey of reconstruction, let us carry forward the lessons etched into our hearts and minds. Let us remember that we are not defined by our losses, but by our capacity to rise above them. Embracing the power of forgiveness, the pursuit of deferred dreams, the resilience that sustains us, and the enduring flame of hope that lights our way, we stand on the threshold of new beginnings.

The road ahead may be uncertain, but it is also filled with potential, and in that potential, we find the essence of our humanity – the capacity to rebuild, to transform, and to thrive.

Chapter Seven
Becoming A Voice For Change

In the aftermath of adversity, there comes a pivotal moment where one's experiences can transcend personal boundaries and become a catalyst for broader societal change. This chapter delves into that transformative process, examining how the trials and tribulations of a personal experience can ignite a passion for advocacy and reform. It's a chapter about evolving from a victim of circumstances to a voice for change, an influencer who can impact lives and reshape societal narratives.

My path to becoming an advocate was neither straightforward nor easy. It required a profound shift in perspective – from seeing myself solely as an individual who had suffered injustice to recognizing the potential impact of my story in the broader context of social justice. This shift was about understanding that the experiences I endured could serve a greater purpose, that my voice could contribute to a dialogue much larger than my own.

The journey to becoming an advocate for change often starts with a deep sense of injustice. For me, this feeling was rooted in the personal experience of wrongful conviction, but it quickly expanded to a recognition of systemic issues within the criminal justice system. This recognition was not just intellectual; it was visceral, born out of the lived experience of navigating a flawed system that often prioritizes expediency over truth.

Embracing the role of an advocate meant channeling the emotions associated with my experiences – the anger, the frustration, the sense of betrayal – into constructive action. It involved moving beyond the realm of personal healing to engage in efforts that could prevent similar injustices from happening to others. This transition from personal recovery to public advocacy is a journey of empowerment, a journey that transforms personal pain into societal gain.

The process of becoming an advocate required me to find my voice, to articulate my experiences and insights in a way that resonated with others. This was not just about recounting my story; it was about connecting my narrative to larger themes of justice, fairness, and human rights. It was about using my story as a tool to illuminate broader issues and to advocate for change.

Finding my voice also meant learning how to navigate public platforms effectively. Whether speaking at events, participating in interviews, or engaging with media, I had to develop the skills to communicate my message clearly and compellingly. This skillset was crucial in amplifying my impact, in reaching audiences that could be mobilized to support the cause of justice reform.

As my journey as an advocate progressed, I came to understand the power of collaboration and partnership.

Working with organizations, activists, and other individuals committed to criminal justice reform allowed me to expand my reach and to contribute to a collective effort that was greater than the sum of its parts. These collaborations were not just strategic; they were deeply enriching, offering new perspectives, insights, and approaches to advocacy.

The path of advocacy also involved educating myself and others about the intricacies of the criminal justice system. This education was essential in identifying the specific areas where change was needed and in developing informed strategies to address these issues. Whether it was understanding the nuances of legal processes, the impact of sentencing policies, or the challenges of reintegration for exonerates, this knowledge became the foundation of my advocacy work.

Engaging in advocacy also meant confronting the challenges and setbacks inherent in the pursuit of systemic change. Change, especially within entrenched systems, is often slow and met with resistance. Navigating these challenges required resilience, patience, and a long-term perspective. It was about staying committed to the cause, even in the face of opposition or slow progress.

Throughout this experience, one of the most profound lessons I learned was the importance of empathy and understanding. Advocacy is not just about advancing a cause; it's about connecting with people, understanding their experiences, and building bridges of understanding and support. Whether it was engaging with other wrongfully convicted individuals, speaking with policymakers, or interacting with the public, empathy was central to my approach.

Becoming an advocate for change also involved embracing a role of leadership. Leadership in advocacy is not about wielding power; it's about inspiring action, guiding efforts, and setting an example of commitment and integrity. It's about being a beacon of hope and a source of strength for those engaged in the struggle for justice.

As my advocacy efforts grew, so did the realization of the broader impact of this work. Advocacy in the realm of criminal justice reform was not just about addressing legal issues; it was about challenging societal attitudes, breaking down stereotypes, and fostering a culture of fairness and compassion. It was about contributing to a movement that sought not only to reform a system but to transform a society.

The journey of becoming a voice for change is a testament to the potential of personal experiences to spark broader societal transformations. It's an experience that demonstrates the power of resilience, the impact of advocacy, and the importance of standing up for what is right. It's a journey that underscores the belief that one person's story can indeed make a difference in the world.

The journey of becoming an advocate for change is like stepping into an entirely new world. It's not just about raising your voice; it's about finding a purpose that resonates deep within your soul. This chapter is all about that transformation, about how your experiences, your hardships, can ignite a fire within you to be a force for positive change, not just for yourself but for the world around you.

For me, this journey wasn't something I set out to do intentionally. It wasn't a plan I had crafted while behind bars, dreaming about the day I would regain my freedom. No, it was something that grew organically out of my experiences, out of the injustice I had faced and the determination to ensure it didn't happen to others.

Becoming an advocate started with a deep sense of injustice. At first, it was personal, rooted in my own wrongful conviction. But as I delved deeper into the world of criminal justice, I began to see the systemic issues that plagued the system itself. It was no longer just about my story; it was about the countless others who had been caught in the same web of injustice.

It was about channeling the anger, the frustration, and the pain into something constructive. It was about moving beyond the hurt and betrayal and using that energy to drive change. It was about realizing that my story, my experiences, could be a tool to shine a light on the flaws in the system.

Finding my voice was a pivotal moment. It meant not just recounting my story but connecting it to larger themes of justice, fairness, and human rights. It was about using my experiences as a lens through which others could see the broader issues at play. It was about speaking in a way that resonated with people, that made them care about the issues I cared about.

But finding your voice is just the beginning. You must learn how to use it effectively. It's about engaging with the public, speaking at events, participating in interviews, and using every platform available to you. It's about learning how to communicate your message clearly and passionately.

Yet, one of the most significant lessons I've learned is that advocacy is not a solitary journey. It's about connecting with others who share your passion. It's about collaborating with organizations, activists, and communities that are already working towards change. It's about recognizing that the collective effort is greater than any individual's.

Education is another critical aspect of advocacy. You must become an expert in your field, understand the nuances of the issues, and be able to propose informed solutions. It's about reading, researching, and staying up to date with the latest developments. Knowledge is your most potent weapon in the fight for change.

But advocacy isn't always smooth sailing. It's a path filled with challenges, setbacks, and moments of doubt. Change, especially in deeply entrenched systems, is often slow and met with resistance. That's where resilience comes in. You must be unwavering in your commitment, even when the road gets tough.

Empathy and understanding are your compass. Advocacy is not about pushing your agenda onto others; it's about fostering constructive dialogue. It's about listening to different perspectives and finding common ground. It's about building bridges rather than burning them.

As you embark on your journey as an advocate, remember that it's not just about pushing for change; it's about being a catalyst for transformation. It's about realizing the potential for impact within your own story, your own experiences. It's about being a force for good in a world that so desperately needs it.

The journey of becoming a voice for change is not just a path of advocacy; it's a profound transformation of the self. It's a journey that teaches you about resilience, empathy, and the power of collective action. It's a journey that shows you how your own experiences, no matter how painful, can be a source of strength and inspiration for others.

As you contemplate your own potential as an advocate for change, remember that the world is filled with opportunities to make a difference. It's not limited to one specific cause or issue. Your voice, your passion, can be channeled into various aspects of life where change is needed, whether it's in your community, your workplace, or your personal relationships.

Take a moment to think about the issues that resonate with you deeply. What injustices, what disparities, what inequalities stir something inside you? What stories, what experiences, can you draw from to connect with others who share your passion for change?

Advocacy is not a solitary endeavor; it's a collective movement. It's about being part of something bigger than yourself, something that transcends the boundaries of your own life. It's about using your voice to amplify the voices of those who may not be heard otherwise.

As you move forward on this journey, remember that becoming a voice for change is not about waiting for the perfect moment. It's about taking that first step, even when you feel uncertain or inadequate. It's about believing in your capacity to make a difference, no matter how small your actions may seem.

So, go out there, speak your truth, and be the change you wish to see in the world. Your experiences, your voice, can be a powerful force for good. The path of advocacy is not always easy, but it is one filled with purpose, impact, and the potential to create a brighter, more just future for us all.

Chapter Eight
The Healing Power Of Forgiveness

In the vast landscape of human emotions, forgiveness stands as a beacon of hope and transformation. It's not a simple act of absolution or a mere gesture of goodwill; it's a profound and intricate journey that has the potential to mend not only broken relationships but also wounded souls. My path toward forgiveness, particularly in the shadow of wrongful conviction and the loss of precious years, was a complex and liberating expedition, guiding me to unexpected realms of inner peace and empowerment.

Forgiveness, as I've come to comprehend it, is more than just a one-time decision; it's an ongoing process that entails letting go of anger, resentment, and the thirst for revenge. It's a journey that commences within, impacting every facet of our existence.

This expedition embarks with the realization that clinging to anger and bitterness serves no constructive purpose. While these emotions are natural reactions to injustice and betrayal, they can become heavy burdens, impeding our capacity to move forward and find serenity. The true challenge, then, lies in transforming these emotions into forces that elevate, rather than diminish, our spirit.

In my own voyage toward forgiveness, the first step was to acknowledge the pain and anger that I harbored towards those who had wronged me. This acknowledgment was crucial as it permitted me to confront these emotions openly and honestly. It was about granting myself the permission to feel, to grieve, and to express the depth of my hurt.

The subsequent phase involved understanding how these emotions had affected my life. I came to realize that my anger, though justifiable, was akin to a heavy chain that shackled me to the past. It was an impediment that prevented me from fully embracing the present and looking toward the future with hope and optimism. This realization was a turning point, a moment when I began to see forgiveness as a pathway to freedom.

However, forgiveness doesn't entail forgetting or absolving the wrongs that were done. It's not about downplaying the gravity of the injustice. Instead, it's about relinquishing the hold that these past events have on our lives. It's about reclaiming our power and agency, choosing to live a life defined not by what happened to us, but by how we respond to it.

The process of forgiveness delves deeply into empathy and understanding. It entails attempting to see the situation from multiple perspectives, to understand the complexities and the fallibilities that characterize human behavior. This doesn't excuse the actions of those who wronged us, but it provides a context that makes forgiveness more attainable.

69

As I journeyed through the intricate process of forgiveness, I found that one of the most challenging and vital aspects was self-forgiveness. Self-forgiveness involves releasing the self-directed anger and blame that we often harbor. It's about accepting that, despite our best efforts, there are things beyond our control, and our worth and identity are not defined by the injustices we have experienced.

This self-forgiveness was nothing short of liberating. It created a space for self-compassion and self-acceptance, allowing me to embrace my vulnerabilities and recognize my strength and resilience. It was a pivotal step in healing and in reconstructing a sense of self that was whole and at peace.

The path toward forgiveness also had a profound impact on my relationships with others. It enabled me to interact with the world from a place of understanding and compassion rather than from one of hurt and suspicion. It fostered a sense of connection and empathy, enabling me to build healthier, more meaningful relationships.

Additionally, forgiveness played a pivotal role in my advocacy work. It granted me a unique perspective on criminal justice reform, one rooted in empathy and understanding rather than vengeance. It enabled me to engage constructively with these issues, contributing to healing, both for myself and for others.

As I embraced the power of forgiveness, I ventured into the spiritual dimensions of this journey. Forgiveness, in many ways, is a spiritual practice. It involves transcending the ego, connecting with inner peace, and tapping into a wellspring of love and compassion that resides within each of us.

This spiritual exploration wasn't about adhering to a specific religious doctrine; rather, it was about connecting with a deeper part of myself. A part capable of immense love, understanding, and grace. It was about finding a source of strength and guidance that transcended the material world.

Forgiveness also brought with it a sense of empowerment. It was empowering to choose forgiveness over resentment, to choose peace over turmoil, and to choose love over hatred. It reaffirmed my ability to shape my emotional landscape and choose the values and principles that would guide my life.

Nonetheless, forgiveness is not a one-time act; it's a continual process, one that demands ongoing effort and commitment. There were moments of doubt, moments when old wounds resurfaced, and the temptation to succumb to anger and bitterness would reappear. But these moments were opportunities to deepen my practice of forgiveness, to reaffirm my commitment to this path.

Let us reflect on the healing power of forgiveness. It's a power that can transform our lives, liberating us from the past and opening us to a future filled with possibility and hope. It's an experience that challenges us to be our best selves, to embrace our humanity with all its complexities, and to live with a heart that is open and free.

For some, forgiveness can be easier said than done, particularly in the face of certain circumstances. It's a process that can be as intricate as it is transformative. What if you find yourself unable to forgive? What if the wounds run too deep, and the scars too permanent? These are valid questions, and it's essential to recognize that forgiveness is not a one-size-fits-all solution. It's a personal journey, and everyone's path may look different.

For those struggling to forgive, the first step is acknowledging that forgiveness is not a moral obligation or a societal expectation. It's a choice, and it's okay if you're not ready to make that choice. Healing takes time, and sometimes, it may require professional guidance or therapy to navigate the complexities of forgiveness.

One approach that can help is reframing the concept of forgiveness. Instead of viewing it as condoning the wrongs that were done, think of forgiveness as an act of self-compassion. By forgiving, you're releasing yourself from the burden of carrying anger and resentment. It's a gift you give to yourself, not to the person who wronged you.

Another crucial aspect is setting boundaries. Forgiveness doesn't mean you have to reconcile with the person who hurt you or put yourself in a vulnerable position again. You can choose to forgive while maintaining distance and protecting yourself from further harm. Boundaries are essential for self-preservation and can coexist with forgiveness.

It's also helpful to seek support from trusted friends, family, or support groups. Sharing your feelings and experiences with others who have faced similar challenges can be incredibly validating. They can offer insights, empathy, and guidance on your journey toward forgiveness.

Journaling is another effective tool. Writing down your thoughts and emotions can provide clarity and help you process your feelings. It's a safe space to express your anger, sadness, and confusion. Over time, journaling can reveal patterns in your emotions and thoughts, allowing you to work through them more effectively.

Mindfulness and meditation practices can assist in calming the emotional storm that often accompanies unforgiveness. These practices can help you stay grounded in the present moment, reducing rumination on past events. They promote self-awareness and self-compassion, which are integral to forgiveness.

In some cases, seeking professional therapy or counseling may be necessary. Therapists can guide you through the process of forgiveness, helping you explore your emotions, identify barriers, and develop strategies for letting go of resentment. Therapy provides a safe and supportive environment for healing.

Ultimately, forgiveness is a personal journey, and there is no deadline or prescribed timeline. It's okay if forgiveness takes years or even a lifetime. The most important thing is to prioritize your well-being and healing.

Whether you ultimately choose to forgive or not, your path is valid, and your experiences are a part of your unique story.

Remember that forgiveness is not a destination but a process. It's not about erasing the past but finding a way to move forward with a lighter heart. It's about releasing the grip that the past has on your present and future. And it's about embracing the possibility of healing, growth, and transformation, no matter how long that journey may take.

As we conclude this exploration of the healing power of forgiveness, remember this: forgiveness is not a gift you give to those who have wronged you; it's a gift you give to yourself. It's a choice to let go of the heavy burden of anger and resentment that can weigh down your spirit. It's a pathway to inner peace, healing, and empowerment.

Forgiveness is not about condoning the actions of others or dismissing the pain they've caused. It's about recognizing that holding onto anger and bitterness doesn't serve your well-being. It's about acknowledging that your worth and identity are not defined by the injustices you've endured.

By forgiving, you're not saying that what happened was okay; you're saying that you deserve to be free from the shackles of the past. You're choosing to release yourself from the grip of anger and to embrace a future filled with hope and possibility. You're opting for a life that's defined by your capacity for love, compassion, and resilience.

In the chapters ahead, we'll continue to explore various aspects of the human experience, from the pursuit of deferred dreams to the process of transforming pain into empowerment. We'll delve into the resilience that sustains us through life's challenges and the hope that guides us toward a brighter future.

The healing power of forgiveness is a reminder that, even in the face of injustice and betrayal, you have the capacity to choose a path of healing and growth. It's an invitation to let go of what no longer serves you and to embrace a life that is defined by compassion, understanding, and self-compassion.

Whether you've already embarked on your journey of forgiveness or are just beginning to consider it, know that you are not alone. Many have walked this path before you, and many will follow. Your experiences, your choices, and your capacity for forgiveness have the potential to inspire others and create a ripple effect of healing and transformation.

As you reflect on this chapter and its insights into forgiveness, remember that forgiveness is a gift you give to yourself—a gift that allows you to reclaim your power, heal your soul, and move forward with a heart that is open, free, and capable of boundless love.

The journey of forgiveness is just one part of your story, and it's a part that can lead to a future filled with peace, purpose, and profound personal growth. Embrace this path with an open heart, and may it bring you the healing and liberation you deserve.

Chapter Nine
Chasing Deferred Dreams

In the intricate tapestry of life, dreams are the threads that weave our ambitions into reality, illuminating the path to our deepest desires. But what happens when these dreams are forcibly deferred, pushed aside by circumstances beyond our control? My journey, marred by wrongful conviction, stands as a testament to the tenacity of the human spirit in the face of such adversity. This chapter is not a mere catalog of discoveries; it's a narrative of how I resurrected those dreams, fueled by a renewed sense of purpose and determination.

Losing my dreams was akin to losing a piece of my identity, an integral part of who I was. Ten years behind bars stripped me of not just my freedom, but of the opportunities I had meticulously crafted. The most prominent among them was a promising football career, a scholarship that promised a future bathed in the neon lights of the NFL.

The journey toward recapturing my dreams began with a heavy sigh of acceptance—the acceptance that my life's trajectory had taken a sharp, unexpected detour. It was a process of acknowledging the profound sense of loss and displacement, a mourning for the dreams I had envisioned.

But acceptance was merely the prologue; the true tale lay in what came after—how I converted that acceptance into a driving force, transforming the pain of deferred dreams into an unshakable determination to reignite the flames that once burned so brightly.

Rediscovering my dreams was an active, conscious endeavor. It meant diving deep into the well of my passions, rekindling the flames that had once fueled my spirit. It was about revisiting old interests and exploring new ones, breathing life into dormant aspirations, and allowing the potential of a vibrant future to unfold.

In this exploration, I learned the art of adaptability—the malleability of dreams. Though my football dreams had been temporarily deferred, they had not vanished; they had evolved, adopting new forms and trajectories. Welcoming this evolution was the key to my progression, embracing the potential for growth and fulfillment in realms unexplored.

Pursuing these reimagined dreams was a process of setting fresh goals—short-term and long-term milestones that constituted a map guiding my journey. These goals weren't merely checkpoints for external achievement; they were steppingstones to personal growth, markers on the path to becoming the person I needed to be to realize my dreams.

Chasing deferred dreams was no jaunty escapade. It was a journey marked by daunting challenges and unanticipated setbacks, moments when doubt clouded the horizon, and the path ahead appeared obscured. Yet, it was precisely in these moments that my resolve, my unyielding commitment, was tested most profoundly.

Perseverance, the unrelenting pursuit of my dreams in the face of seemingly insurmountable odds, became my most potent ally. It was the fuel that stoked the fires of hope, even in the darkest hours. It stood as a testament to the indomitable spirit of human resilience, a reminder that our dreams are worth the relentless effort and unwavering dedication required to bring them to fruition.

As I ventured on the odyssey of pursuing deferred dreams, I discovered the immeasurable value of support and mentorship. Surrounding myself with those who believed in my potential, who provided guidance, encouragement, and wisdom, was pivotal to my progress. These individuals weren't just allies; they were partners in my quest, comrades who shared in my struggles and rejoiced in my triumphs.

The pursuit of deferred dreams also entailed daring risks, stepping out of the familiar and embracing the uncharted. It was about having the audacity to try, to experiment, to stumble, and to rise anew. This willingness to take calculated risks was not an act of recklessness; it was a testament of faith—faith in my own abilities and faith in the transformative power of the journey itself.

As I pursued my dreams, I also learned the art of patience. Dreams, especially those long deferred, are not realized overnight. They demand time, effort, and unwavering commitment. Patience, in this context, was not synonymous with passivity; it was a recognition that meaningful achievements are worth the wait, that the journey to realizing our dreams is as meaningful as the destination itself.

In the heart of this experience, a profound realization dawned on me—the intricate interplay of dreams and identity. Our dreams reflect our innermost selves, a mirror that reflects our values, passions, and aspirations. Pursuing them is not merely about accomplishing a set of goals; it is an act of self-expression, a commitment to living a life in alignment with our deepest convictions.

This epiphany was empowering. It reinforced my belief in the power of personal agency, in the ability to shape one's destiny, and in the capacity to transcend adversity. It was a reaffirmation that our dreams, even when deferred, possess the potential to redefine our lives and reshape our identities.

As I embarked on the journey of chasing deferred dreams, I seized the opportunity to inspire others. Sharing my story, my trials, and my victories became a conduit for motivating others to pursue their own dreams, to embrace the prospect of a brighter future. It was about transforming my experiences into a wellspring of hope and encouragement for those who crossed my path.

The path of chasing deferred dreams is an enduring testament to the resilience of the human spirit. It is a narrative that challenges us to never relinquish our aspirations, to persist unwaveringly in the face of adversity, and to believe unreservedly in our potential to surmount obstacles. It is a voyage that underscores the beauty of dreaming, the exhilaration that accompanies the pursuit of our passions, and the fulfillment that flows from realizing our fullest potential.

Contemplate the pursuit of deferred dreams as an ode to human resilience, courage, and the transformative potency of ambition. Reflect on how the pursuit of your own dreams can be a voyage of personal growth and self-discovery, a sojourn that leads to a future teeming with potential and promise.

The pursuit of deferred dreams takes on an extraordinary significance when we consider individuals like Yusef Salaam and Jarrett Adams, whose stories serve as powerful testaments to the resilience of the human spirit. In their journeys, we find inspiration that transcends the ordinary, reminding us that dreams can be recaptured even after the darkest of nights.

Yusef Salaam, an Exonerated "Central Park Five" member, is a remarkable example of turning tragedy into triumph. His life's path took a devastating turn when, as a teenager, he was wrongly imprisoned in connection to the infamous 1989 rape and beating of a white jogger in Central Park. For almost seven years, Salaam bore the weight of an unjust conviction. But he refused to let the darkness of his circumstances snuff out the light of his dreams.

Two decades later, DNA evidence surfaced, shedding a glaring light on the miscarriage of justice that had befallen him and four other Black and Latino men. Their convictions were overturned, and the truth came to the surface, a truth that exposed not only the fallibility of the legal system but the indomitable strength of the human spirit.

Yusef Salaam's story took a remarkable turn when he decided to step into the realm of politics, winning a New York City Council seat. Poised to represent a central Harlem district, his candidacy stands as a symbol of transformation and the power of dreams. Salaam's journey from wrongful imprisonment to the halls of city politics serves as a powerful reminder that dreams deferred can indeed be reignited, and that resilience and determination can overcome the most daunting of odds.

Jarrett Adams, another beacon of hope in the realm of wrongful convictions, had to traverse a path laden with obstacles to chase his dreams. Falsely convicted of a crime he did not commit, Adams found himself behind bars, his freedom stripped away unjustly. It was within the confines of his prison cell that he began his quest for justice, a quest that would ultimately lead him to discover the profound flaws within the legal system.

As an innocent man navigating the labyrinthine complexities of the legal system, Adams was forced to become his own advocate. He had to learn the intricacies of the law to secure his own release, an arduous journey that would forever alter the course of his life. What he uncovered along the way were not just the cracks in the system but chasms of injustice that ensnared countless innocent citizens.

Adams emerged from his ordeal with a profound sense of purpose. He recognized the need for reform, for a legal system that would safeguard the rights and liberties of all individuals, especially the innocent. Armed with the knowledge he had acquired during his struggle for freedom, he dedicated his life to advocating for change within the legal system, becoming an attorney and a beacon of hope for others who had suffered similar injustices.

These stories of Yusef Salaam and Jarrett Adams are not just tales of personal triumph but lessons in the enduring power of dreams. They remind us that, even in the face of grievous injustice, the human spirit can rise above adversity and find renewed purpose. They exemplify how the pursuit of dreams can become a catalyst for profound change, not just in the lives of individuals but in society at large.

As we reflect on their journeys, we are invited to consider the dreams we may have deferred in our own lives, the aspirations that may have been pushed aside by circumstances beyond our control. The stories of Salaam and Adams encourage us to rekindle those dreams, to chase them with unwavering determination, and to recognize that, even in the darkest of times, our dreams can be our guiding stars, leading us toward a brighter and more purposeful future.

As we conclude this chapter on the pursuit of deferred dreams, I want to leave you with a resounding message of hope and empowerment. The stories of Yusef Salaam and Jarrett Adams, along with my own journey, are living proof that dreams, no matter how long they've been deferred, can still become a radiant reality.

In my own life, I refused to surrender to the darkness of wrongful imprisonment. I held onto the dream of playing in the NFL, and I pursued it relentlessly. Against all odds, I achieved that dream, proving that resilience, faith, and unwavering determination can propel us to heights we once thought were unattainable.

Yusef Salaam and Jarrett Adams stand as beacons of hope, their experiences reminding us that injustice can be overcome, and the pursuit of justice can lead to transformative change. They transformed their pain into purpose, their adversity into advocacy, and their dreams into realities.

So, I implore you, dear reader, to never give up on your dreams. Your aspirations, no matter how long they've been deferred or how challenging the journey may seem, are worth chasing. Embrace the spirit of resilience, take bold steps forward, and remember that the pursuit of your dreams is a testament to the strength of the human spirit.

As you embark on your own journey of chasing deferred dreams, know that you are not alone. There is a community of dreamers, advocates, and believers who stand with you. Seek out the support and mentorship of those who share your vision, and let their guidance illuminate your path.

In the chapters to come, we will continue to explore the transformative power of hope, resilience, and the pursuit of a brighter future. We will delve into the resilience that sustains us through each step, the process of transforming pain into empowerment, and the hope that guides us toward a future filled with possibility and change.

So, as you contemplate your own dreams and aspirations, remember that the pursuit of those dreams is not just a personal endeavor; it is a journey of collective inspiration. Your dreams have the potential to ignite positive change in your life and the lives of others. Embrace them with unwavering determination and let them be the guiding stars that lead you to a future rich with purpose and passion.

In the words of Langston Hughes, "Hold fast to dreams, for if dreams die, life is a broken-winged bird that cannot fly." Keep your dreams alive and let them carry you to heights you've never imagined. The pursuit of deferred dreams is a testament to the resilience of the human spirit, and your journey is a part of that remarkable tapestry of hope and possibility.

Chapter Ten
Transforming Pain into Empowerment

In the crucible of life's toughest challenges, where pain and adversity meld, there lies an extraordinary opportunity for transformation. My journey, marked by wrongful conviction and the ensuing emotional and mental anguish, serves as a testament to this profound transformation. As we embark on this final part of our expedition, let me share with you my experience and insights into how we can turn the pain of injustice into a catalyst for empowerment.

When you've been wrongfully convicted, the pain is unlike any other. It's not just the loss of freedom, though that's a heavy burden to bear. It's the loss of time, opportunity, and trust – a cascading series of losses that leave you feeling like a shipwrecked soul in a vast ocean of despair. My wrongful conviction stole from me not just years of my life, but also my dreams, my reputation, and my sense of security in the world.

I had dreams of playing in the NFL, dreams of making my family proud, and dreams of a future filled with promise. But those dreams were ripped away from me, replaced by the harsh reality of a prison cell. The emotional and mental toll of that experience was immeasurable. It felt like I was trapped in a never-ending nightmare, a nightmare where the truth was a distant echo drowned out by the clamor of a flawed justice system.

In those dark days, it would have been easy to succumb to the pain, to let it define me, to let it extinguish the spark of hope that still flickered deep within. But that's not what I chose. Instead, I made a conscious decision to confront my pain, to understand it, and ultimately, to transform it into a source of strength and empowerment.

The first step in this transformation was self-awareness. I had to acknowledge the depth of my pain and the injustice that had been done to me. It was not a sign of weakness but a necessary act of courage. I had to face the demons of anger, bitterness, and despair that threatened to consume me. By acknowledging the pain, I took control of it, rather than letting it control me.

Empowerment through pain involves more than just self-awareness; it requires empathy and community. I was fortunate to have a support system that believed in my innocence, but I also witnessed the suffering of fellow inmates who were also wrongfully convicted. Their stories, their pain, became intertwined with mine. In sharing our experiences, we found solace and strength in each other's company. We became a community bound by a common struggle, and that sense of solidarity was a powerful force.

Another crucial aspect of this transformation was reframing my narrative. Instead of seeing myself solely as a victim of injustice, I began to view myself as a survivor and a fighter. I refused to let the wrongful conviction define me. I started to see the opportunity within the challenge, the chance to become a voice for change and a beacon of hope for others who were also trapped in the darkness of wrongful convictions.

Acting and advocating for justice became integral to my journey. I didn't want my pain to be in vain; I wanted it to serve a purpose. So, I used my experience to shine a light on the flaws in the justice system, to raise awareness about wrongful convictions, and to advocate for reform. It was a way of channeling my pain into a force for positive change.

As we explore further in this chapter, we'll delve into the ways in which pain can be transformed into empowerment. My experience, along with those of other exonerees, offers valuable insights into the resilience of the human spirit and the potential for growth even in the face of the most profound injustices.

One of the most inspiring aspects of this transformation is witnessing the incredible resilience of individuals who have faced wrongful convictions. They refuse to be defined solely by their past, and instead, they use their experiences as a catalyst for change.

Take the case of Gloria Killian, a woman who spent 17 years in prison for a crime she did not commit. Her wrongful conviction was a harrowing ordeal that could have easily broken her spirit. However, Gloria chose a different path. She emerged from prison not as a victim, but as an advocate for criminal justice reform.

During her time behind bars, Gloria not only fought for her own exoneration but also connected with other inmates who had experienced injustices. She became a source of support and hope for those around her, helping them navigate the challenges of the criminal justice system.

Upon her release, Gloria channeled her pain and frustration into a relentless pursuit of justice reform. She became an outspoken advocate for the wrongfully convicted, using her own story as a powerful example of the flaws in the system. Gloria's transformation from a wrongfully convicted inmate to a crusader for change is a testament to the human capacity for resilience and empowerment.

Her story reminds us that, even in the darkest of circumstances, there is the potential for growth, advocacy, and making a positive impact on the world. Gloria's dedication to reforming the criminal justice system serves as an inspiration to all who face adversity, showing that pain can be transformed into a force for change.

As we continue our exploration in this chapter, we'll delve deeper into the ways in which individuals like Gloria, and many others, have harnessed their pain to become advocates, champions of justice, and beacons of hope for a more equitable society. Their stories illuminate the path from suffering to empowerment, offering valuable lessons for us all.

As we journey through the transformative process from pain to empowerment, it's crucial to recognize that this path is not exclusive to those who have faced wrongful convictions. It is a journey that each one of us, in our own unique way, can embark upon to navigate the challenges and adversities life presents. The transformation we seek begins with understanding the power of our own resilience and our capacity to overcome obstacles.

Let's talk about F.E.A.R. - False Evidence Appearing Real. Fear is often the shadow that looms large over our aspirations and endeavors. It's that inner voice that whispers doubts and insecurities, making obstacles seem insurmountable. It is, in essence, the false evidence that appears real in our minds.

The first step in overcoming fear is to recognize it for what it is - a product of our thoughts and perceptions. It's the stories we tell ourselves about the challenges we face, the doubts we harbor, and the limitations we impose on ourselves. Fear is not an objective reality; it's a subjective interpretation of reality.

Understanding this is liberating because it means we have the power to change our perception. We can reframe fear as an opportunity for growth, a challenge to be met, rather than an insurmountable barrier. By doing so, we transform fear from an obstacle into a steppingstone on our path to empowerment.

Next, we must confront fear with courage. Courage is not the absence of fear but the willingness to act despite it. It's about taking that first step, even when our knees are shaking, and our hearts are racing. Courage is the catalyst that propels us forward on the journey of transformation.

To navigate this transformation effectively, it's essential to set clear goals. What do you want to achieve? What does empowerment look like for you? Setting specific, achievable goals provides a roadmap for your journey. It helps you stay focused and motivated, even in the face of adversity.

Moreover, surrounding yourself with a supportive community can make a world of difference. Just as exonerees find strength in advocacy groups and supportive networks, having people who believe in your potential can be a tremendous source of encouragement. Seek out individuals who share your vision, who can offer guidance and support as you navigate your own path.

But remember, the journey of transformation is not without its challenges. There will be setbacks, moments when fear creeps back in, and doubts resurface. In these moments, it's essential to practice resilience. Resilience is the ability to bounce back from adversity, to learn from failures, and to keep moving forward.

Embrace your setbacks as opportunities for growth. Every stumble is a chance to learn, adjust your course, and come back even stronger. It's a reminder that transformation is not a linear path; it's a series of ups and downs, but it's in those downs that we often find our greatest strengths.

Lastly, don't underestimate the power of self-compassion. Treat yourself with kindness and understanding, just as you would a friend facing a challenge. Self-criticism and self-doubt only feed fear and hinder transformation. Instead, practice self-compassion as you navigate this journey. You deserve your own support and encouragement.

In conclusion, the transformation from pain to empowerment is a path we all can tread, regardless of our circumstances. It's about recognizing fear for what it is, confronting it with courage, setting clear goals, seeking support, practicing resilience, and extending self-compassion. Remember, fear is just False Evidence Appearing Real, and you have the power to transform it into the fuel that propels you toward your own empowerment.

As you continue your journey, embrace the challenges, celebrate the victories, and keep moving forward. The transformation you seek is not only possible; it's within your grasp. The power to overcome obstacles and achieve empowerment lies within you.

With courage, resilience, and a compassionate heart, you can navigate this transformative path and emerge stronger, wiser, and more empowered than ever before. So, fear not, for you have the tools to conquer it and to transform your life in remarkable ways.

As we conclude this chapter and our exploration of transformation from pain to empowerment, there's a fundamental truth that I want to impress upon you: no one will work harder for you than you. This journey is about your pursuit of peace, happiness, success, and empowerment, and it's a journey that requires your unwavering commitment and effort.

I've learned through my own experiences that true transformation begins with a decision, a choice to take control of your life and your destiny. It's about acknowledging that you have the power to shape your own future, regardless of the challenges you may face. No external force, no matter how well-intentioned, can replace the determination and effort that come from within.

Resilience is the bedrock of this journey. It's the quality that allows you to bounce back from setbacks, to weather the storms of life, and to keep moving forward. Resilience is not just a trait; it's a skill that can be developed and honed over time. It's about learning to adapt to adversity, to find strength in moments of weakness, and to view obstacles as opportunities.

In my own life, I've faced immense challenges, from the wrongful conviction that stole my freedom to the uphill battle of reclaiming my dreams. Resilience was my constant companion, the inner fire that kept me going even when the odds seemed insurmountable. I learned that setbacks were not failures but steppingstones on the path to success.

It's important to understand that the journey of transformation is not without its difficulties. There will be moments when fear creeps in, when self-doubt threatens to derail your progress. But it's in these moments that your resilience shines brightest. It's when you summon the courage to face your fears head-on, to challenge your doubts, and to persevere despite the odds stacked against you.

Throughout my life, I've met countless individuals who, like me, have faced seemingly insurmountable challenges and have emerged stronger and more empowered. Their stories are a testament to the human spirit's capacity for resilience and transformation. They remind us that no matter how dire the circumstances, we have the power to rise above them.

The pursuit of peace, happiness, success, and empowerment is not a linear journey. It's a series of peaks and valleys, each offering its own lessons and opportunities for growth. It requires patience and perseverance. It demands that you stay committed to your goals, even when the path ahead is uncertain.

As you navigate this journey, it's important to set clear and achievable goals. What does peace look like for you? What does happiness mean to you? What does success and empowerment entail in your life? Define these goals with clarity, for they will serve as your guiding stars, illuminating the path forward.

Surrounding yourself with a supportive community is equally crucial. Seek out individuals who believe in your potential, who can offer guidance and encouragement when the going gets tough. The power of a supportive network cannot be overstated; it can provide the strength and motivation you need to persevere.

Furthermore, remember that setbacks are not indicators of failure but opportunities for growth. Embrace them as valuable lessons that will propel you forward. Every obstacle you overcome, every challenge you face, is a testament to your resilience and your commitment to transformation.

In my own life, I've seen how resilience can transform adversity into advantage. It's not about avoiding difficulties but about harnessing them as sources of strength. It's about recognizing that the journey itself is transformative, shaping you into a stronger, more empowered individual.

As we conclude this chapter and look ahead to the journey that lies before you, I want you to carry with you the knowledge that you have the power to transform your life. You have the resilience to face adversity and emerge stronger. Your pursuit of peace, happiness, success, and empowerment is not a distant dream; it's a reality within your grasp.

With unwavering commitment, resilience, and the belief in your own potential, you can navigate this transformative path and create a life that reflects your deepest aspirations. No one will work harder for you than you, and no one is better equipped to shape your destiny.

So, as you continue your journey, remember these words: You are resilient, you are capable, and you are empowered to transform your life in ways you may have never imagined. The path may be challenging, but with each step forward, you are moving closer to the peace, happiness, success, and empowerment that you seek.

Onward, dear reader, with the knowledge that you have the inner strength to overcome any obstacle and to create a life that is rich with fulfillment and purpose. Your journey is a testament to the resilience of the human spirit, and I have no doubt that you will achieve the transformation you desire.

Chapter 11
Building A Legacy of Change and Hope

In the tapestry of life, each thread we weave carries the potential to leave an indelible mark, shaping not just our destiny but also the fabric of society itself. As we stand at the confluence of personal transformation and societal impact, this chapter embarks on a journey to explore the concept of legacy. It is about transcending the bounds of individual experience to sow seeds of change and hope for generations to come. My journey, marked by trials, resilience, and empowerment, serves as a beacon, illuminating the path towards building a legacy that resonates with the ethos of justice, compassion, and progress. This chapter is not just a culmination of my story but a bridge to the future, where each step, each decision, and each triumph contributes to a lasting legacy of change and hope.

Defining a legacy is a deeply introspective process, one that calls us to reflect on the essence of our life's work and its ripple effects in the world. For me, a legacy is not just about the memories and achievements left behind; it is about the enduring impact of our actions on the lives of others and the world at large. It's about how our journey through darkness and adversity lights a path for others, offering guidance, inspiration, and a vision for a better future. A legacy born from overcoming wrongful conviction extends beyond personal vindication; it encompasses a commitment to transforming the justice system, inspiring resilience in others, and nurturing a society that upholds truth and fairness. As we delve into this concept, we aim to unravel the threads of experiences, choices, and values that weave together to form a legacy that transcends time and circumstance.

The impact of a legacy on future generations is profound and far-reaching. In crafting our legacy, we must consider how our actions and teachings will shape the minds and hearts of those who follow in our footsteps. It involves not only imparting lessons learned from personal struggles but also instilling values that will guide future generations in their own quests for justice and fulfillment. This is especially pivotal when considering the legacy left by those who have traversed the rocky terrain of wrongful conviction. The lessons imparted can ignite a passion for justice, a commitment to ethical integrity, and a resolve to challenge and reform flawed systems. By sharing our stories, we become architects of a future where such injustices are less likely to occur, laying the foundation for a more equitable and compassionate society.

The continuation and sustainability of advocacy efforts are crucial in ensuring that the impact of one's legacy endures. Advocacy, especially in the realm of criminal justice reform, is not a sprint but a marathon, requiring persistence, resilience, and adaptability. The challenge lies in keeping the momentum alive, in continually igniting passion and commitment within us and others. It is about finding innovative ways to engage, educate, and empower new generations of advocates who will carry the torch forward. This means creating platforms for dialogue, fostering collaborative networks, and developing resources that equip and inspire future changemakers. In doing so, we ensure that the legacy of advocacy, born from personal pain and struggle, becomes a perpetual force for positive change in the world.

In the heart of my journey lies a story of transformation – from a life marred by injustice to a life dedicated to advocacy and reform. This transformation is not just a personal triumph but a beacon for others navigating similar adversities. My legacy, therefore, is intertwined with the stories of those I inspire and support. It's about creating a pathway for others to follow, a trail blazed through the thicket of challenges I've overcome. This legacy is embodied in every speech I deliver, every article I write, and every conversation I have about the deep-seated issues within our justice system. It's a legacy that seeks to empower others to take up the mantle of advocacy, to be voices for the voiceless, and to contribute to a world where justice prevails over prejudice.

As we explore the legacy we leave for future generations, we must consider the profound power of education and awareness. Education, in this context, extends beyond the confines of traditional learning. It encompasses the dissemination of knowledge about our legal system's intricacies, the sharing of personal stories that humanize the often faceless victims of wrongful conviction, and the promotion of critical thinking about the societal structures that enable such injustices. By fostering a culture of informed awareness, we empower future generations to identify, challenge, and rectify systemic flaws. This educational legacy is pivotal in shaping a more discerning and empathetic society, one capable of driving progressive change and safeguarding the rights of all its members.

Collaboration and partnership are fundamental in amplifying the impact of our advocacy and ensuring the longevity of our legacy. Working alongside other reformers, legal professionals, community leaders, and activists allows us to pool our resources, knowledge, and influence. This collective approach not only strengthens our efforts but also creates a synergistic impact greater than the sum of its parts. It's about building alliances that transcend individual pursuits, fostering a unified front against injustice. Such collaborations serve as a testament to the power of unity in driving societal change, reinforcing the idea that together, we are stronger and more capable of enacting lasting reform.

The personal narrative I've reframed – from victim to advocate – is not unique to my journey alone. Countless individuals have turned their experiences of adversity into powerful platforms for advocacy and reform. Their stories, much like mine, underscore the transformative power of resilience and determination. For instance, consider the plight of those who have been wrongfully incarcerated. Each story is a unique tapestry of pain, struggle, and eventual triumph. These narratives, when shared, become more than personal recollections; they transform into rallying cries for justice, equality, and reform. They inspire, they educate, and most importantly, they galvanize action, compelling others to join in the fight against systemic injustice.

My experience has taught me that the essence of a meaningful legacy often lies in the willingness to take calculated risks and step into uncharted territories. Embracing the unknown, with its inherent uncertainties and potential setbacks, is a testament to true courage. In my journey, this meant stepping beyond the comfort of personal healing and into the arena of public advocacy and policy influence. It involved sharing my story with a broader audience, challenging entrenched beliefs, and advocating for tangible changes in the criminal justice system. This aspect of my legacy is not just about personal redemption; it's about setting a precedent for bravery and initiative that inspires others to take bold steps for the causes they believe in. It's a legacy that speaks to the heart of change-making, encouraging future generations to not shy away from challenges but to embrace them as opportunities for growth and impact.

Alongside risk-taking, the pursuit of a legacy is inextricably linked to the art of patience and the virtue of persistence. True change, especially in systems as complex and resistant as the criminal justice system, is rarely instantaneous. It requires a steady, unwavering effort, often in the face of daunting obstacles and prolonged periods of seemingly little progress. My path to advocacy has been a marathon, not a sprint, marked by small victories and occasional setbacks. But each step forward, no matter how small, is a crucial part of the journey. This legacy of patience and persistence serves as a guiding light for others, demonstrating that meaningful change is a cumulative process, built over time through consistent effort and unwavering dedication.

A significant component of building a legacy involves fostering an environment of empathy and understanding – virtues that are often overshadowed in the pursuit of justice. Through my advocacy, I've strived to create a dialogue that transcends mere legal discourse, reaching into the realm of human experience and emotion. It's about crafting narratives that touch hearts, change minds, and open eyes to the realities of injustice. This empathetic approach to advocacy seeks to bridge divides, build mutual understanding, and create a more compassionate society. It's a legacy that values the power of human connection, recognizing that at the core of our quest for justice is the fundamental need for empathy and understanding in our interactions with one another.

The process of transforming pain into empowerment is not a solitary endeavor but a collective journey. It's about joining hands with those who share similar experiences, who understand the depths of injustice, and who are equally committed to creating change. In my advocacy, I have found strength in numbers – in the collective voices of exonerees, activists, and allies. Together, we have formed a chorus of change, each voice amplifying the message of reform and resilience. This aspect of my legacy is about the power of community and solidarity, highlighting that even the most profound transformations are often the result of collective efforts, shared struggles, and united visions.

In cultivating a legacy, one must also consider the broader societal implications of their actions and advocacy. The ripples of change we create extend far beyond our immediate circle, influencing communities, shaping policies, and altering societal narratives. For me, this meant not just addressing the immediate concerns of wrongful convictions but also engaging in conversations about the broader aspects of justice, fairness, and human dignity. It's about recognizing our role as part of a larger ecosystem where each action can contribute to a more just and equitable society. This legacy is not confined to the realms of law and justice; it encompasses a commitment to societal wellbeing and moral responsibility, urging future generations to think critically about the kind of world they wish to inhabit and shape.

Reflecting on my journey, I realize that the transformation from pain to empowerment, and the subsequent creation of a legacy, is imbued with moments of profound introspection and self-discovery. It involves delving into the depths of one's character, confronting personal limitations, and emerging with a renewed sense of purpose and clarity. This journey of self-discovery is as much about understanding oneself as it is about influencing others. It's about aligning one's values, actions, and goals in a way that not only brings personal fulfillment but also serves the greater good. In this sense, building a legacy is an ongoing process of personal evolution, where each experience, each challenge, and each triumph contributes to a richer, more nuanced understanding of oneself and one's place in the world.

An integral part of building a legacy is the willingness to mentor and guide others who are embarking on similar paths. The knowledge and insights gained from my experiences are not merely personal assets; they are tools for empowerment that can be shared with others. Through mentorship, I have the opportunity to nurture the next generation of advocates and leaders, passing on lessons of resilience, advocacy, and ethical integrity. This aspect of legacy-building extends the scope of my journey, ensuring that the wisdom gleaned from my experiences transcends my personal story and contributes to the growth and development of others. It's about planting seeds for a future where informed, compassionate, and courageous individuals continue the work of building a just and empathetic world.

Looking forward, the concept of legacy prompts us to consider the enduring impact of our actions. It's about envisioning a future where the fruits of our labor continue to flourish long after we are gone. This forward-looking perspective is not just about setting goals for the immediate future; it's about considering the long-term effects of our advocacy and actions. It's about building something sustainable and impactful, something that stands the test of time and continues to inspire and effect change. In this sense, building a legacy is akin to planting a forest – it requires patience, care, and the understanding that the full extent of its growth and impact may only be realized in years to come.

As we near the conclusion of this chapter, and indeed our journey, the emphasis shifts to the tangible actions and initiatives that embody the essence of a lasting legacy. It's about translating vision into reality, ideals into practice. This means actively engaging in community projects, policy advocacy, educational programs, and other endeavors that have a direct impact on societal well-being and justice. My involvement in these areas is not just a contribution to the present; it's an investment in the future, a way to ensure that the values of fairness, empathy, and resilience are ingrained in the fabric of our society. This practical aspect of legacy-building is a call to action, urging us not only to dream of a better world but to take concrete steps towards creating it.

In reflecting upon the journey thus far, it becomes evident that building a legacy is an ever-evolving process. It adapts with time, grows with experience, and is continually shaped by the challenges and triumphs encountered along the way. My story, marked by wrongful conviction and the fight for justice, is but one chapter in a larger narrative of human resilience and societal progress. It serves as a reminder that each of us has the power to contribute to this narrative, to add our unique voice and efforts to the collective endeavor of shaping a more just and compassionate world. The legacy I aspire to leave is one that not only reflects my personal journey but also resonates with the aspirations and struggles of countless others who seek justice and empowerment.

As this chapter – and our collective journey – draws to a close, it is my hope that the insights and experiences shared here serve as a catalyst for each reader to contemplate their own legacy. What will be the mark you leave on the world? How will your experiences, challenges, and triumphs contribute to the tapestry of societal change and human progress? The pursuit of a meaningful legacy is not reserved for a select few; it is a possibility that exists for each one of us. It begins with the choices we make, the values we uphold, and the commitment we show towards realizing our vision for a better world. I encourage you, the reader, to embrace this pursuit with passion, determination, and an unwavering belief in your ability to make a difference.

In closing, let us remember that the journey of transforming pain into empowerment, of chasing deferred dreams, and of building a legacy, is a testament to the indomitable human spirit. It is a journey that speaks to our inherent capacity for resilience, creativity, and compassion. As you move forward in your own journey, carry with you the lessons learned, the inspiration gained, and the resolve to create a positive and enduring impact. May your legacy be a beacon of hope, a source of inspiration, and a catalyst for change, echoing through the corridors of time and touching the lives of generations to come. Onward, with courage and conviction, to a future where our collective efforts culminate in a legacy of change, hope, and enduring empowerment.

Chapter Twelve
Embracing the Journey Ahead - A Conclusion

As we draw the curtains on this explorative journey, it is essential to revisit and crystallize the essence of resilience that has been the backbone of this narrative. Resilience, as we've discovered, is not merely the ability to withstand adversity; it is a multifaceted strength that encompasses growth, adaptability, and the courage to face life's unpredictability. Throughout this book, we've seen resilience manifest in various forms - from the grit in confronting wrongful conviction to the perseverance in advocating for justice. This resilience is more than a personal attribute; it's a beacon that guides us through dark times, offering hope and a promise of renewal. As we reflect on these stories, we understand that resilience is not inherent but cultivated through challenges, making us not only survivors but also harbingers of change.

Building upon this foundation, we then ventured into the realm of turning personal injustice into a force for societal advocacy, a theme that resonates deeply in our journey. The transition from a victim of circumstance to an agent of change is a profound metamorphosis, marked by an awakening to the power of one's voice and actions. The chapters dedicated to this transformation highlighted not just the struggle against the odds but also the triumph in influencing and reshaping societal narratives. This part of our journey emphasizes the importance of using our experiences, however harrowing, as catalysts for broader change, inspiring others to join in creating a more just and empathetic world.

Forgiveness, a theme that we explored with depth and sensitivity, deserves a moment of revisitation in our concluding reflections. Forgiveness, as we learned, is not about absolving wrongdoers, or diminishing our pain, but about liberating ourselves from the shackles of bitterness and resentment. It's a transformative process that allows us to move forward with a lighter heart, paving the way for healing and inner peace. In the context of our journey, forgiveness is a vital step towards empowerment, enabling us to redefine our narratives from being defined by our past to being shaped by our aspirations and values.

Chasing and realizing deferred dreams has been a recurring motif in our narrative, symbolizing hope and the indomitable human spirit. The pursuit of dreams deferred by wrongful conviction or other life-altering events is a testament to our capacity for rebirth and reinvention. This pursuit is not just about the realization of specific goals but about the journey itself - a journey marked by resilience, self-discovery, and the reclamation of lost parts of our identity. It's a powerful reminder that our dreams, no matter how long delayed, hold the key to a fulfilling and purpose-driven life.

Embracing the journey ahead, we recognize that the path of transformation is not a solitary trek but one enriched by the presence and support of others. Throughout our narrative, the role of community and connection has emerged as a cornerstone of resilience and empowerment. In our shared struggles and triumphs, we find strength and solidarity. This sense of community transcends individual experiences, creating a tapestry of collective resilience. It's in these connections that we find not only empathy and understanding but also the collaborative energy necessary to effect meaningful change. As we forge ahead, let us remember the value of these connections, cherishing and nurturing the relationships that empower us and those around us.

Our journey also highlights the importance of transforming pain into empowerment, a theme that resonates with profound significance. Each chapter has illustrated that pain, while an inevitable part of life, can be a powerful catalyst for growth and change. This transformation is not about denying or escaping our hardships but about redefining our relationship with them. It's about channeling our struggles into purposeful action, turning our scars into symbols of strength. This alchemy of the spirit is not just a personal triumph but a beacon of hope for others, showcasing the limitless potential of the human soul to overcome and thrive.

As we look towards the future, we must also acknowledge the ongoing nature of this transformative journey. The path to resilience and empowerment is not linear nor finite; it is a continuous process of learning, growth, and adaptation. Our stories do not end with the closing of this book; they are but chapters in a larger, evolving narrative. Each step forward, each challenge overcome, and each dream realized contributes to our ongoing development. This journey demands persistence, patience, and an enduring commitment to our core values and goals. It invites us to remain open to new experiences, to embrace change, and to continually seek out opportunities for personal and collective evolution.

This journey reminds us that the legacy we leave is crafted not only by our achievements but also by the resilience we demonstrate, the compassion we show, and the connections we foster. Our legacy is defined by how we navigate our challenges, how we impact those around us, and how we contribute to the world we live in. As we conclude this chapter and reflect on the journey we've undertaken, let us carry forward the lessons learned, the inspiration garnered, and the resolve to continue making a positive impact. Our journey is a testament to the power of the human spirit and its capacity to transform adversity into opportunity, pain into strength, and dreams into realities.

In envisioning the path forward, it becomes imperative to embrace a proactive stance towards life's uncertainties and challenges. This proactive approach, a recurrent theme in our narrative, encourages us not just to react to adversities but to anticipate and prepare for them. It's about cultivating a mindset that sees potential where others see problems, and opportunities in places where others perceive obstacles. This approach is not about reckless optimism but about a pragmatic and strategic vision that empowers us to navigate life's complexities with agility and foresight. By adopting this mindset, we not only enhance our resilience but also position ourselves as architects of our own destiny, capable of shaping a future that aligns with our deepest values and aspirations.

Moreover, our journey underscores the significance of embracing lifelong learning as a key component of personal and societal development. The chapters have highlighted that learning is not confined to formal education but is an ongoing process that permeates every aspect of our lives. It involves staying curious, open-minded, and engaged with the world around us. This continuous quest for knowledge and understanding enriches our perspectives, enhances our skills, and keeps us adaptable in an ever-changing world. As we move forward, let us cherish this pursuit of knowledge, recognizing that it is a powerful tool for empowerment and a crucial element in building a legacy of change and hope.

The concept of stewardship also emerges as a pivotal aspect of our journey. Stewardship, in this context, refers to the responsibility we hold towards ourselves, our communities, and future generations. It's about making decisions and taking actions that not only benefit us in the present but also consider their long-term impact. This sense of stewardship extends to how we treat our environment, how we contribute to our communities, and how we influence the world. It calls for a balance between self-interest and the greater good, urging us to act not just as inhabitants of the present but as custodians of the future. Embracing this role of stewardship is essential as we forge a path forward, ensuring that our actions today contribute to a sustainable and equitable world tomorrow.

Finally, as we contemplate the end of this journey, it is essential to acknowledge the role of gratitude in our lives. Gratitude is more than a mere feeling of thankfulness; it is a profound recognition of the blessings, lessons, and opportunities that life presents, even during trials. Embracing gratitude allows us to maintain a balanced perspective, to appreciate the journey we've undertaken, and to recognize the contributions of those who have supported and inspired us along the way. It cultivates a sense of contentment and well-being, providing a foundation for a life marked by fulfillment and joy. As we move forward, let us do so with hearts full of gratitude, mindful of the richness of our experiences and the boundless potential that lies ahead.

As the author and the soul of this narrative, I have walked a path that many would deem unimaginable. Yet, in this journey, one of the most profound lessons I've learned is the power of perspective. It's the lens through which we view our experiences, the filter that colors our world. This journey has taught me that perspective is a choice – a choice to see challenges as opportunities, setbacks as lessons, and adversity as a catalyst for growth. By choosing a perspective that embraces resilience and hope, I've been able to transform my narrative from one of loss and injustice to one of empowerment and purpose. As we move forward, I encourage you to consider your perspective, to recognize it as a powerful tool in shaping your journey and to use it to foster a life of positive impact and meaningful change.

Reflecting on my personal journey, I've come to understand the indispensable role of resilience in navigating the unpredictable waters of life. This resilience, born out of my wrongful conviction and the struggle to reclaim my life, has been a guiding force, illuminating the path through the darkest tunnels. It's a resilience that is not just about enduring but about thriving – about finding ways to grow stronger and more determined with each obstacle. My experience has shown me that resilience is not a static trait but a dynamic process, continually evolving and adapting. It's about being knocked down and having the courage to stand back up, time and again. As you embark on your own journeys, remember that resilience is your companion, a source of strength that empowers you to face life's challenges with courage and grace.

Throughout this narrative, the theme of turning pain into purpose has been a constant echo. My journey from a wrongful conviction to becoming a voice for change is a testament to this transformation. It's about harnessing the pain of injustice and channeling it into advocacy, education, and reform. This transformation is not a path I walked alone; it's a journey shared with countless others who have faced similar adversities. It's about creating a collective voice that advocates for justice, fairness, and compassion. In sharing my story, my aim has been to inspire others to turn their challenges into opportunities for growth and impact. Let this message resonate with you – that pain can be a powerful catalyst, propelling you towards a life of purpose and positive change.

In the pursuit of dreams and aspirations, I've learned the value of perseverance and the importance of holding onto hope. My dream of playing professional football, once seemingly shattered by my wrongful conviction, was reignited by an unwavering belief in possibility and a relentless pursuit of that goal. This journey was not without its challenges, but it was the steadfast commitment to my dreams that fueled my journey forward. It's a reminder that dreams, no matter how deferred, can be realized with determination and persistence. As you chase your own dreams, let my story be a beacon of hope, showing that with perseverance and belief in yourself, even the most distant dreams can be brought within reach.

As we approach the conclusion of this journey, my reflection turns to the essence of what it means to live a life of impact and meaning. This book, a chronicle of my experiences, embodies a fundamental truth: our lives are defined not by what happens to us, but by how we respond to it. The power of human resilience, as showcased in my story, is a testament to our ability to overcome the most daunting challenges. It is a reminder that each of us holds within an incredible capacity for transformation and growth. I implore you, the reader, to harness this power. Let your life be a story of triumph over adversity, a narrative that inspires others and leaves a lasting imprint on the world.

I want to emphasize the importance of hope and the relentless pursuit of a better tomorrow. My journey from the depths of despair in a prison cell to reclaiming my freedom and dreams underscores the indomitable nature of hope. It is the light that guides us through the darkest of times, the anchor that keeps us grounded in the stormiest of seas. Embrace hope in your journey, no matter the challenges you face. Let it be the force that drives you forward, fueling your dreams and aspirations. Hope is not just an emotion; it is a way of life, a choice to believe in the possibility of a brighter future.

As you close this book and reflect on the journey we've shared, consider the legacy you wish to create. Each day offers a new canvas, an opportunity to paint your story, to contribute to the tapestry of life in a way that is uniquely yours. Your actions, your words, your choices – each is a brushstroke in the masterpiece of your life. Strive to make each one count, to live with intention and purpose. Remember, the legacy we leave is not measured by material success or accolades, but by the lives we touch, the change we inspire, and the love we spread. Your legacy is your mark on the world, a reflection of the impact you've made and the difference you've created.

I extend my heartfelt gratitude to you, the reader, for embarking on this journey with me. It has been a path of revelation, healing, and empowerment, not just for me but, I hope, for you as well. My story is a single thread in the vast fabric of human experience, yet it is intertwined with the stories of many. May you find within these pages the inspiration to forge your own path, to overcome your challenges, and to create a life of resilience, purpose, and joy. Go forth with courage and conviction, knowing that within you lies the strength to change your world and, in doing so, to contribute to the betterment of all. Your journey is not just your own; it is a part of a greater story, a resilient echo that reverberates through time, inspiring and empowering others in its wake. Embrace this journey with an open heart and an unwavering spirit, and may your echoes resonate with hope, love, and transformation.

Made in the USA
Las Vegas, NV
22 December 2023

83358374R00069